Wander, Gather, Savor, Ponder

By Katie Daisy

CHRONICLE BOOKS
SAN FRANCISCO

Hallmark

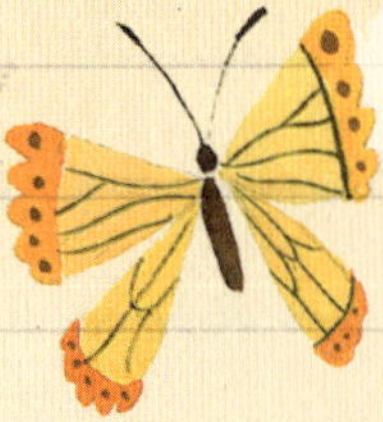

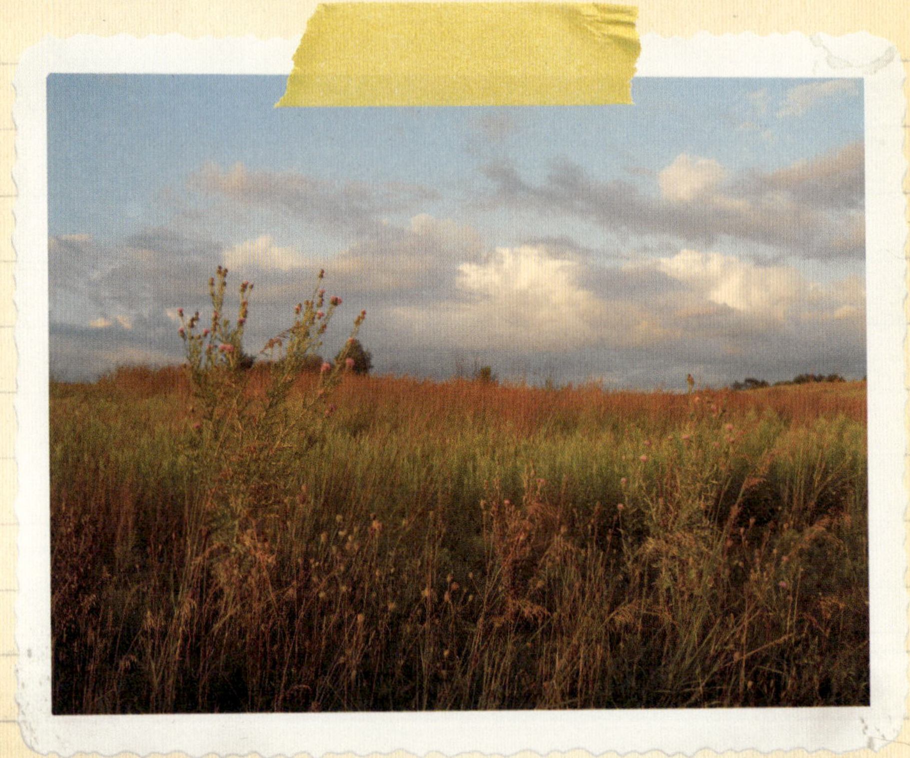

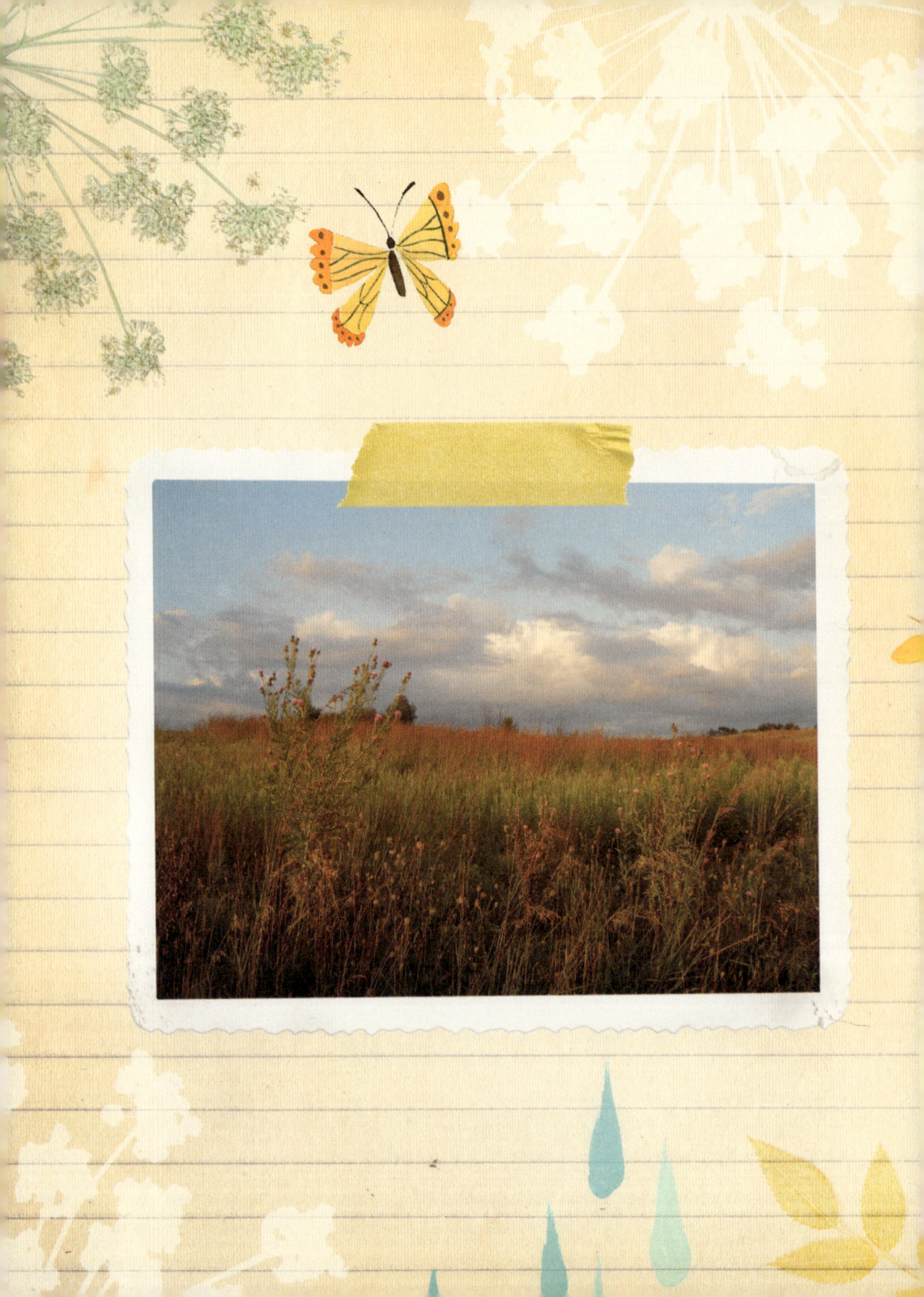

introduction

When you're a child in Lindenwood, Illinois, time does not exist. The summer days are long and full of wonder. Wild daisies line the fence posts, red-winged blackbirds sing songs to the meadow, and tiny toads hide in the tall grass. As the sun sets, the yard becomes dappled with fireflies, the sky dazzles with the brightest of constellations, and the distant coyote howl becomes a lullaby to it all.

I may live two thousand miles from my hometown of Lindenwood, but the wonder of this small town stays with me always. It reminds me that I still have the same eyes I had as a child and can still see the magic that exists everywhere—as long as I take time to wander about the natural world, gather fleeting moments, savor the sweetness, and ponder life's endless offerings of beauty.

I invite you along on this journey with me. So love, look with eyes for seeing beauty, and get out into it.

katie daisy

T Y L O R
Chelsea
Medford
Schultz Siding
Merrill
Cadott
Boyd
WAN

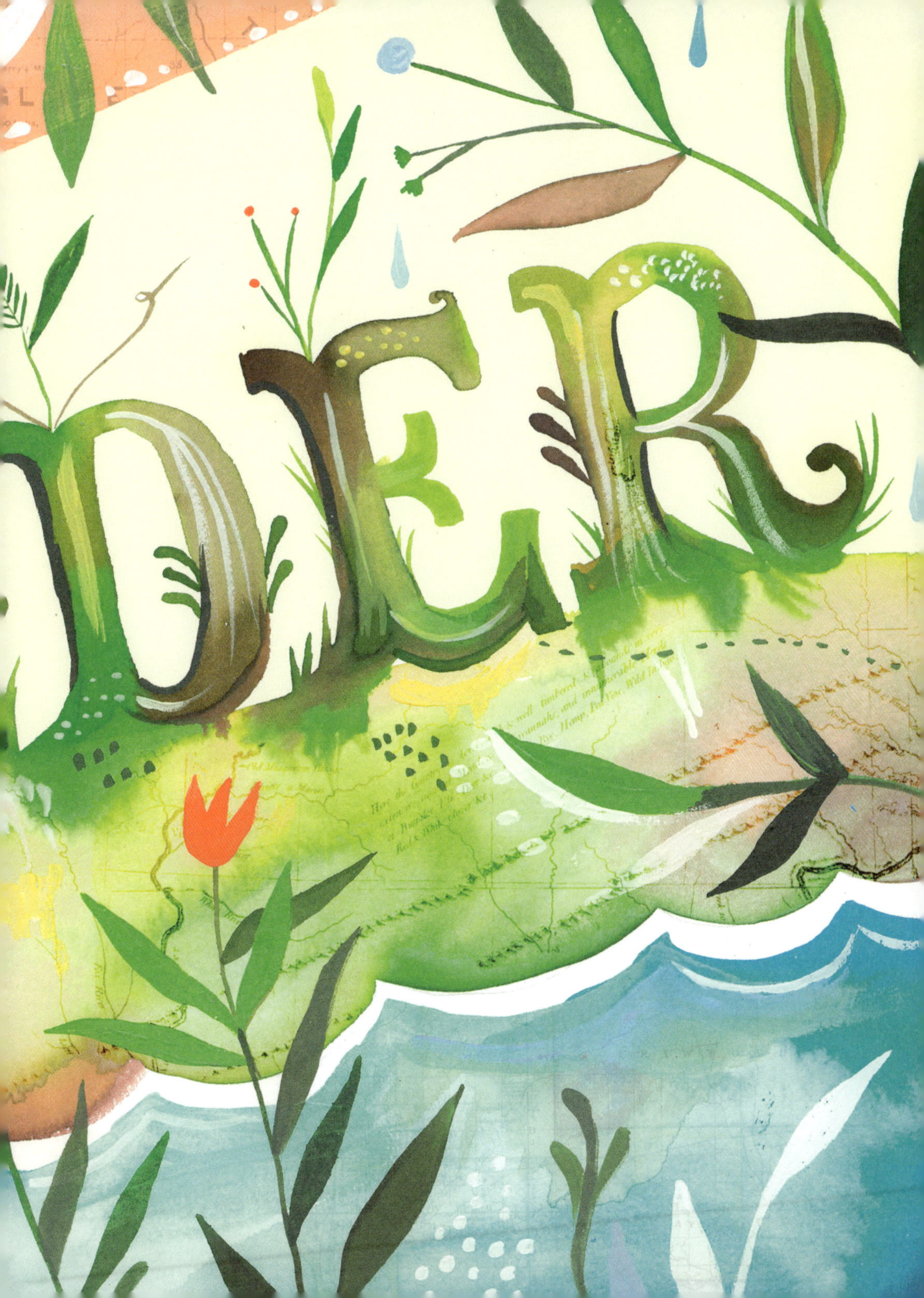
DER

AFOOT AND
LIGHT-HEARTED
I TAKE TO
THE OPEN ROAD,
HEALTHY, FREE,
THE WORLD
BEFORE ME.

—WALT
WHITMAN

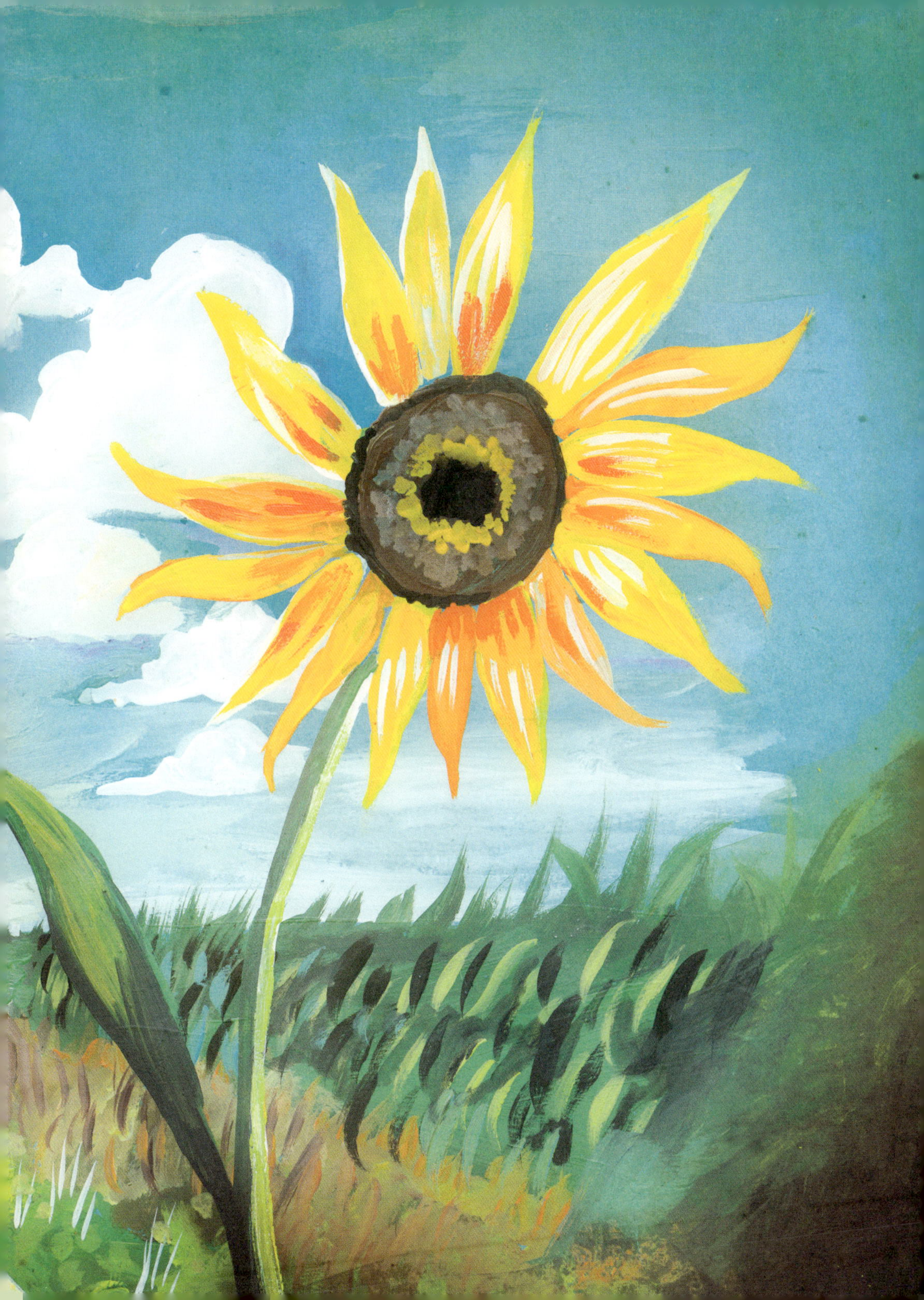

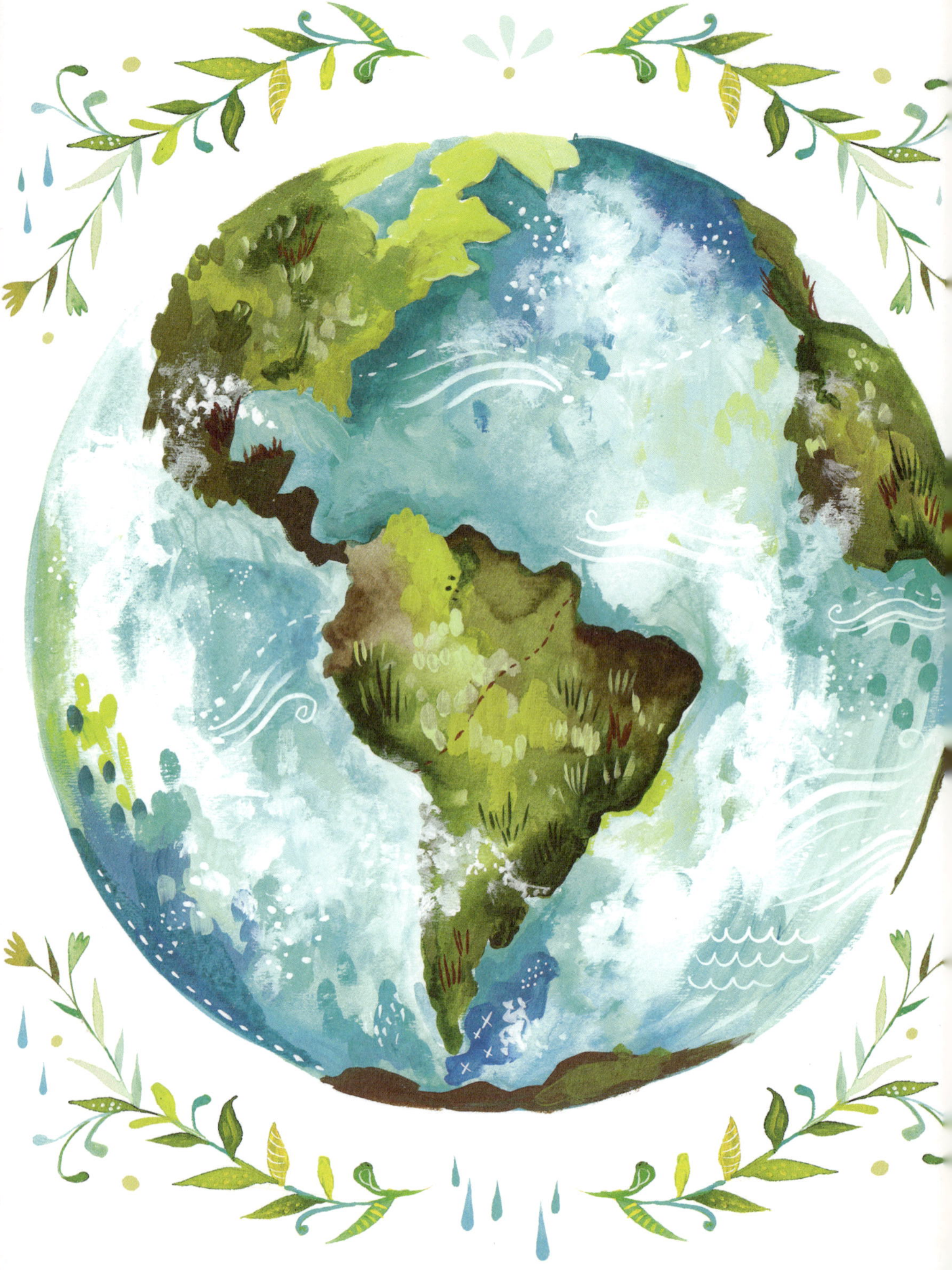

wanderlunch

- peach
- avocado
- baguette
- honey stick
- wedge of cheese
- thermos of tea
- piece of dark chocolate
- handful of almonds

Climb the mountains and get their good tidings. Nature's peace will flow into you as sunshine flows into trees. The winds will blow their own freshness into you, and the storms their energy, while cares will drop off like autumn leaves.

—John Muir

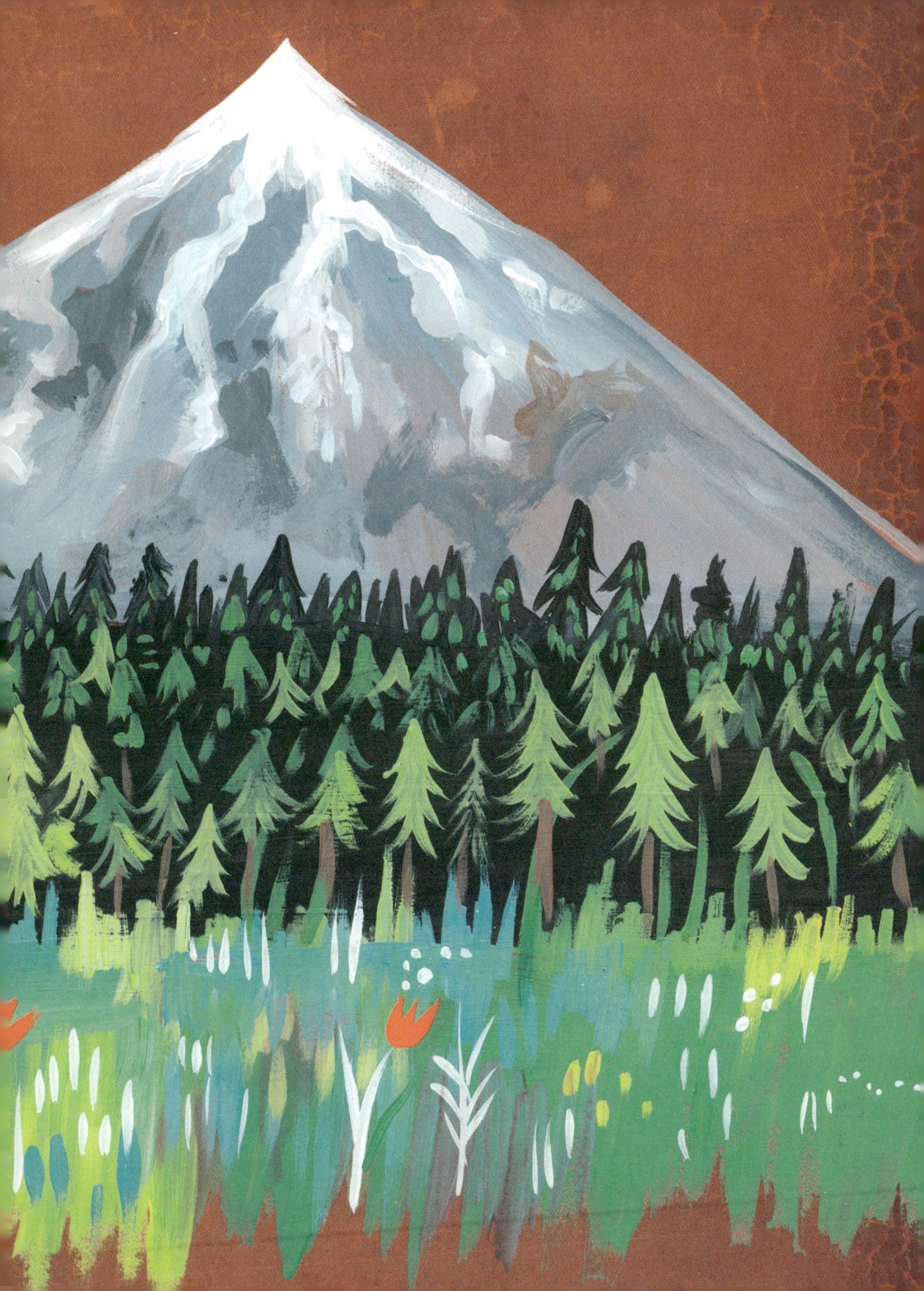

MAGICAL PLACES TO VISIT

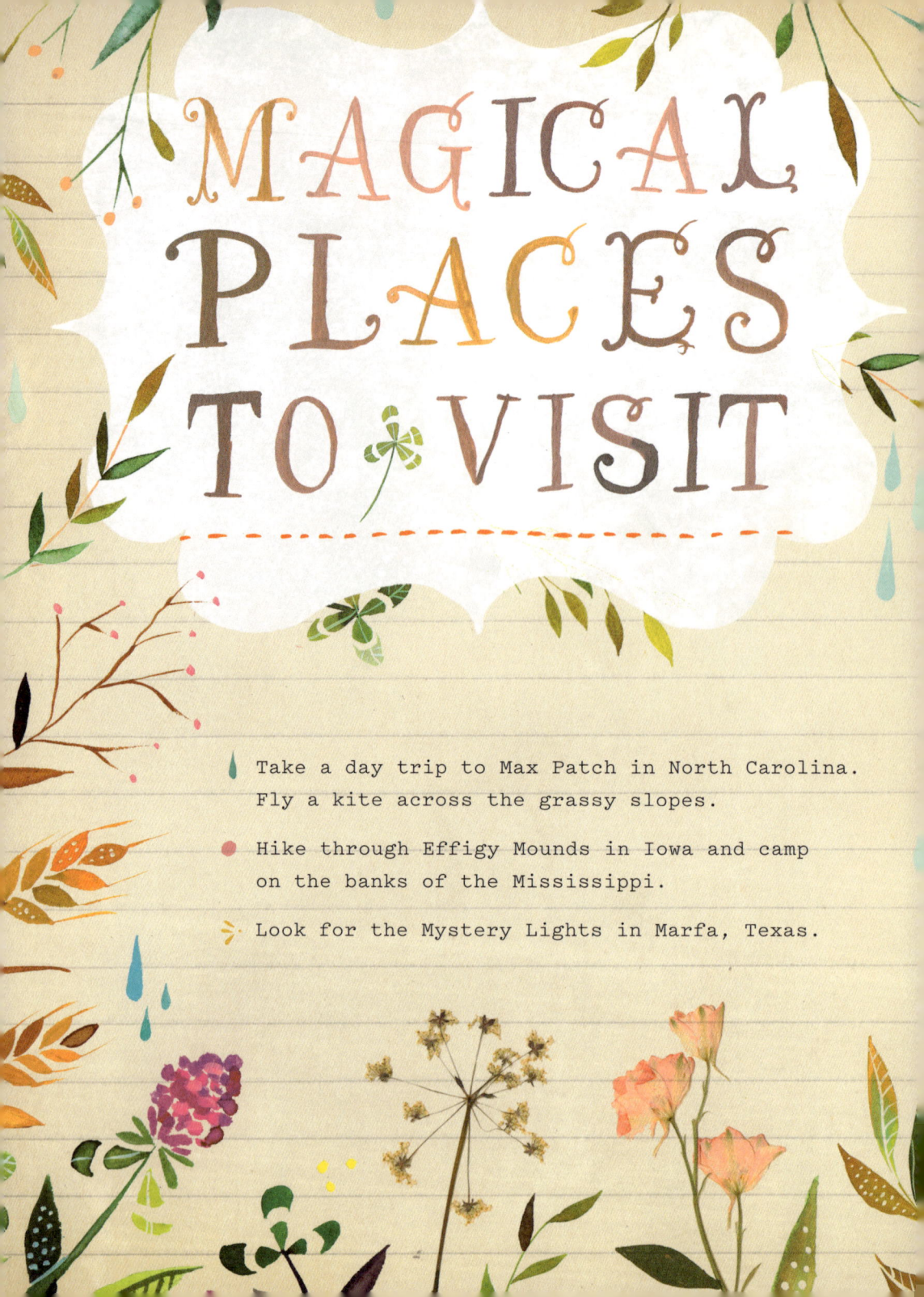

- Take a day trip to Max Patch in North Carolina. Fly a kite across the grassy slopes.
- Hike through Effigy Mounds in Iowa and camp on the banks of the Mississippi.
- Look for the Mystery Lights in Marfa, Texas.

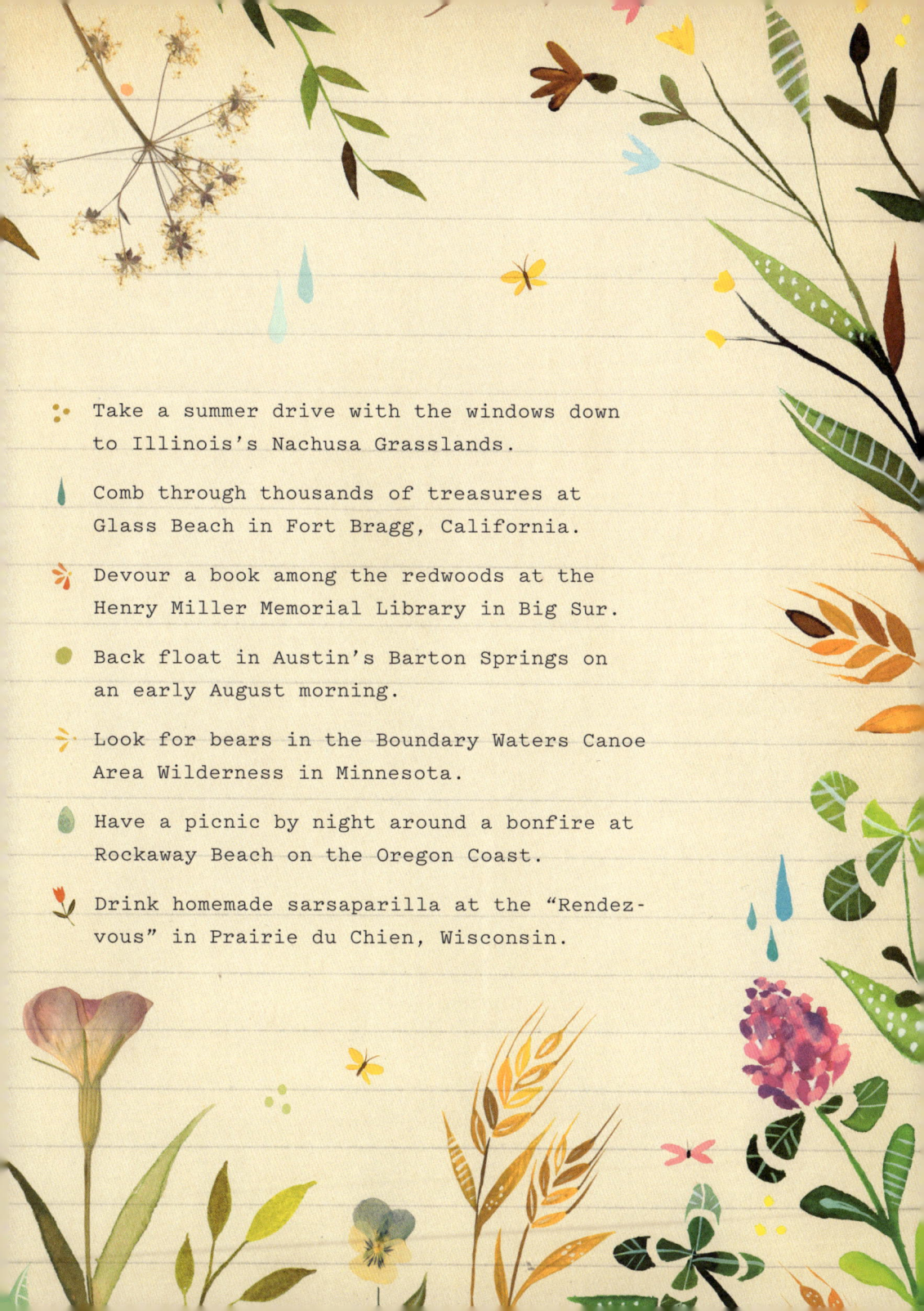

- Take a summer drive with the windows down to Illinois's Nachusa Grasslands.

- Comb through thousands of treasures at Glass Beach in Fort Bragg, California.

- Devour a book among the redwoods at the Henry Miller Memorial Library in Big Sur.

- Back float in Austin's Barton Springs on an early August morning.

- Look for bears in the Boundary Waters Canoe Area Wilderness in Minnesota.

- Have a picnic by night around a bonfire at Rockaway Beach on the Oregon Coast.

- Drink homemade sarsaparilla at the "Rendezvous" in Prairie du Chien, Wisconsin.

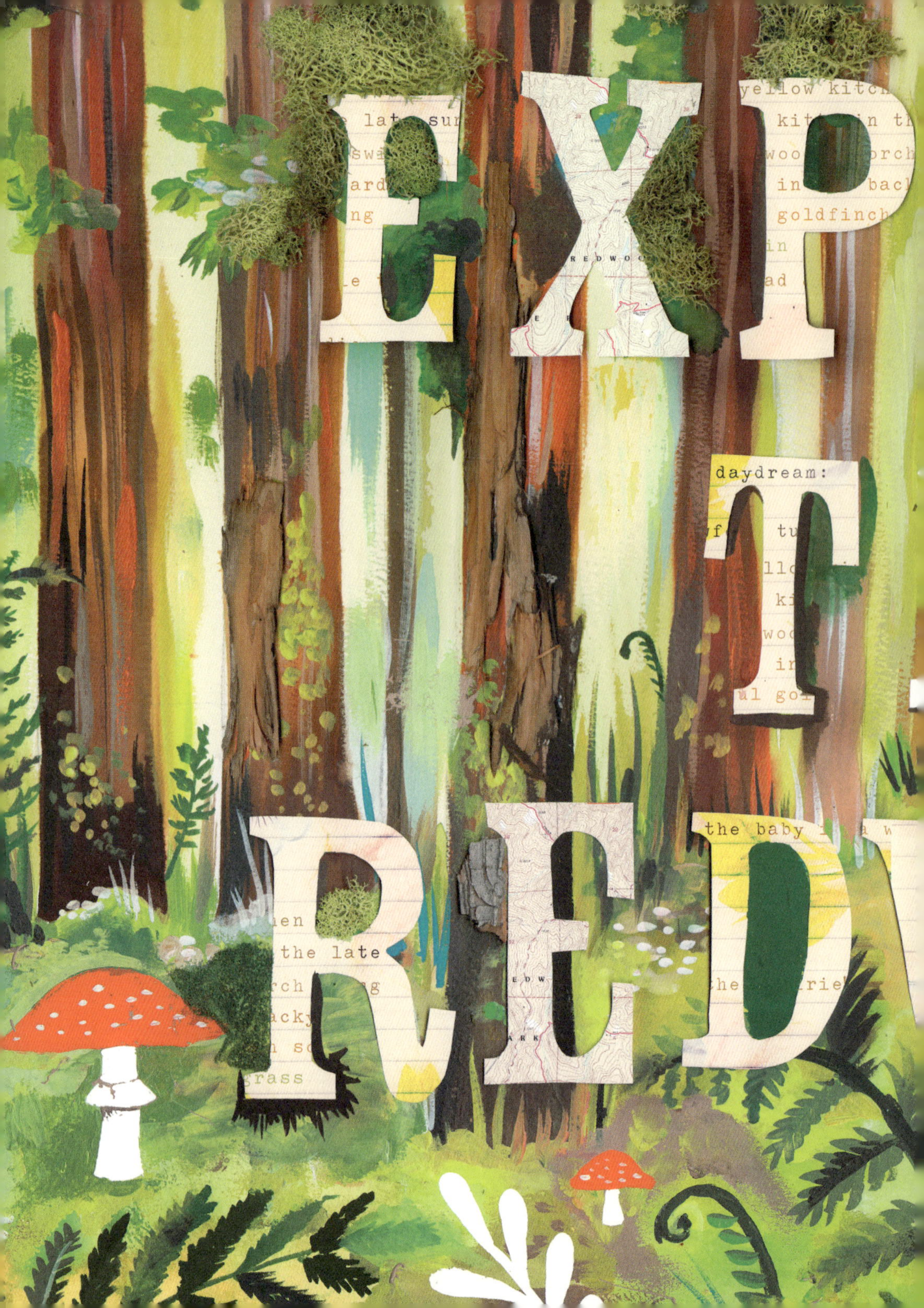

EXP
T
RED
daydream:
goldfinch
the late
the baby

LORE OF THE WOODS

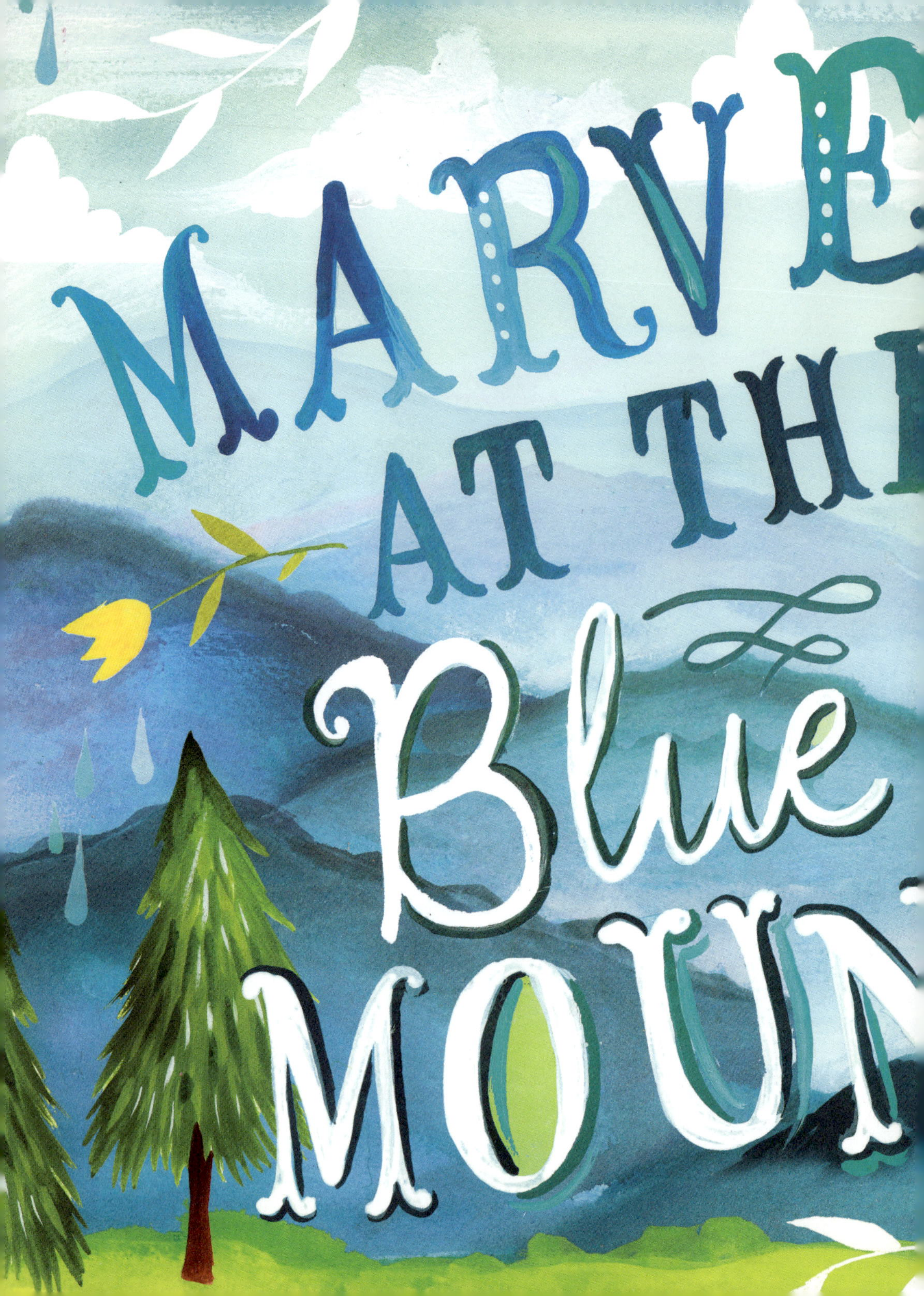
MARVE
AT TH
Blue
MOU

Ridge
TAINS

explore these NATIONAL FORESTS

Superior – MN
Deschutes – OR
Helena – MT
Sequoia – CA
Sierra – CA
Pisgah – NC

comb these **NATIONAL SEASHORES** and **LAKESHORES**

Canaveral – FL
Point Reyes – CA
Apostle Islands – WI
Pictured Rocks – MI
Indiana Dunes – IN

DAYDREAM UNDER

GIANT SEQUOIAS

HIKE
APPAL
TR

THE APPALACHIAN TRAIL

Poisonous Plants

Poison Ivy

Narcissus

Poison Sumac

Lily of the Valley

Poison Oak

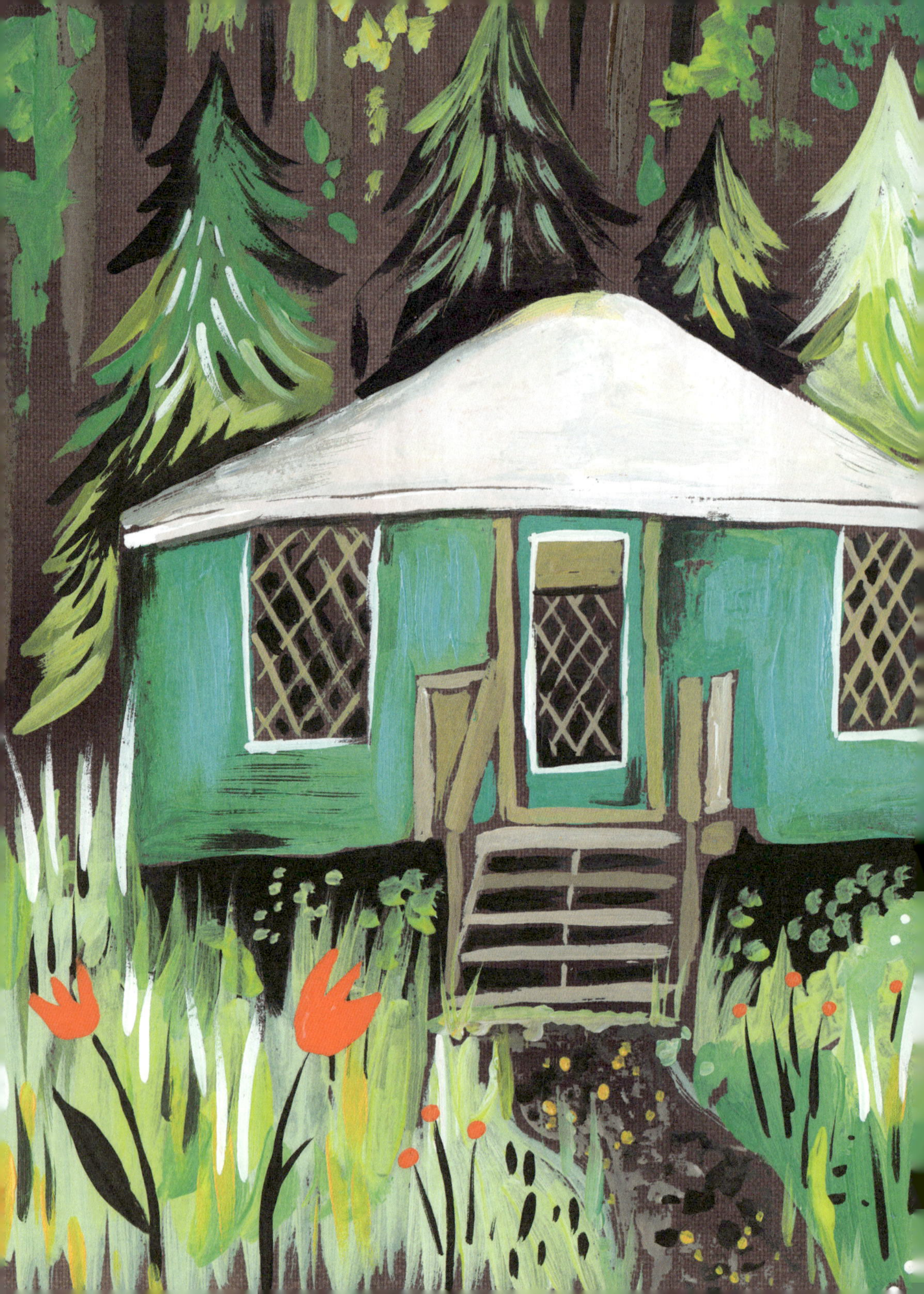

STAY IN A YURT ON THE OCEAN

CREEK SWIMMING AND TANGLED HAIR

TAKE
CROSS
ROAD

COUNTRY TRIP

DRIVE DOWN HIGHWAY 1 WITH THE WINDOWS OPEN.

FEEL THE SALT AIR & WARM BREEZE ON YOUR SKIN.

EXP
BIG

ORE
SUR

GET LOST IN AN UNFAMILIAR TOWN

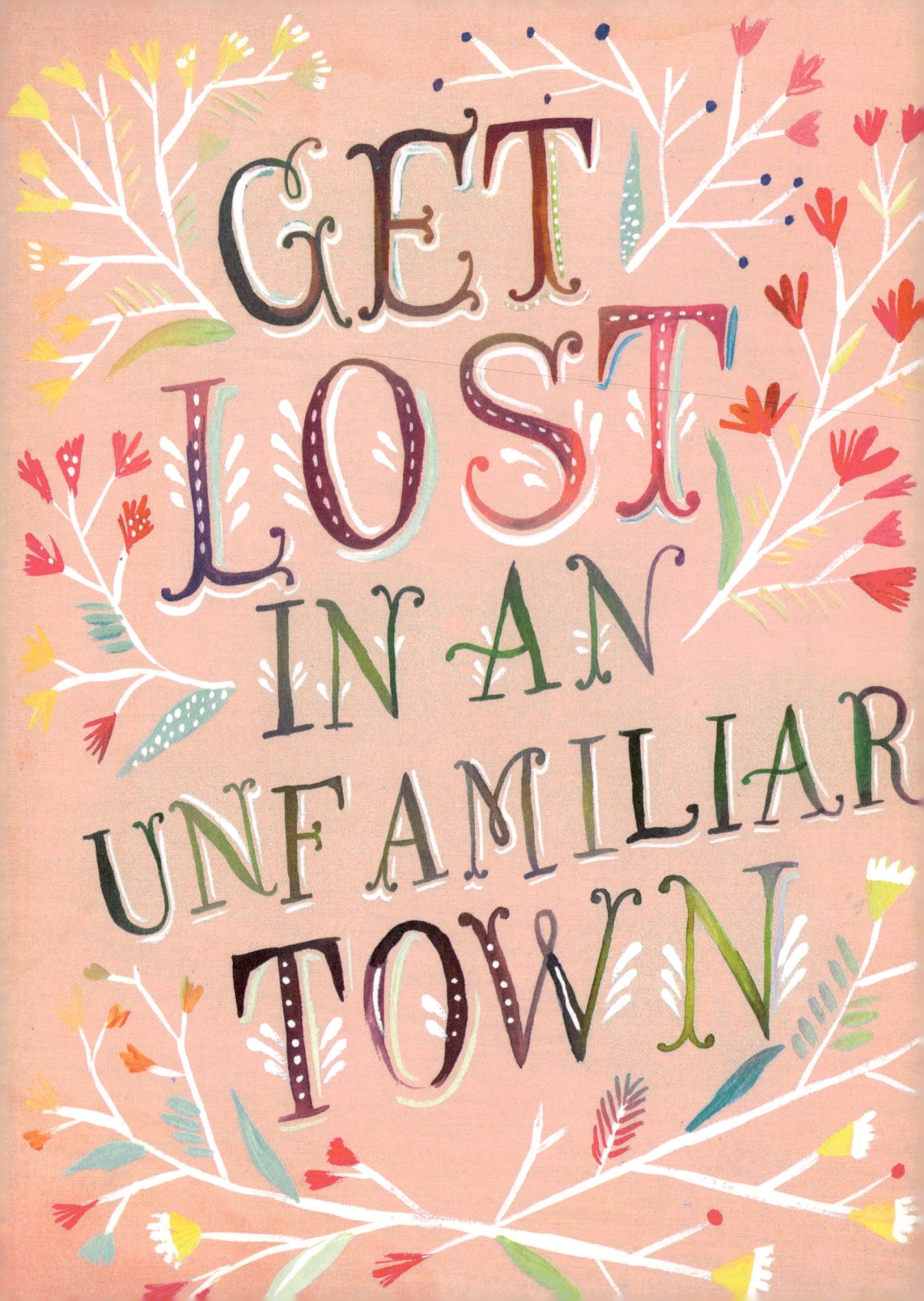

WALNUT, IOWA

YACHATS, OREGON

HARRISON, MAINE

WEAVERVILLE, NORTH CAROLINA

LINDENWOOD, ILLINOIS

MENDOCINO, CALIFORNIA

FALL CREEK, WISCONSIN

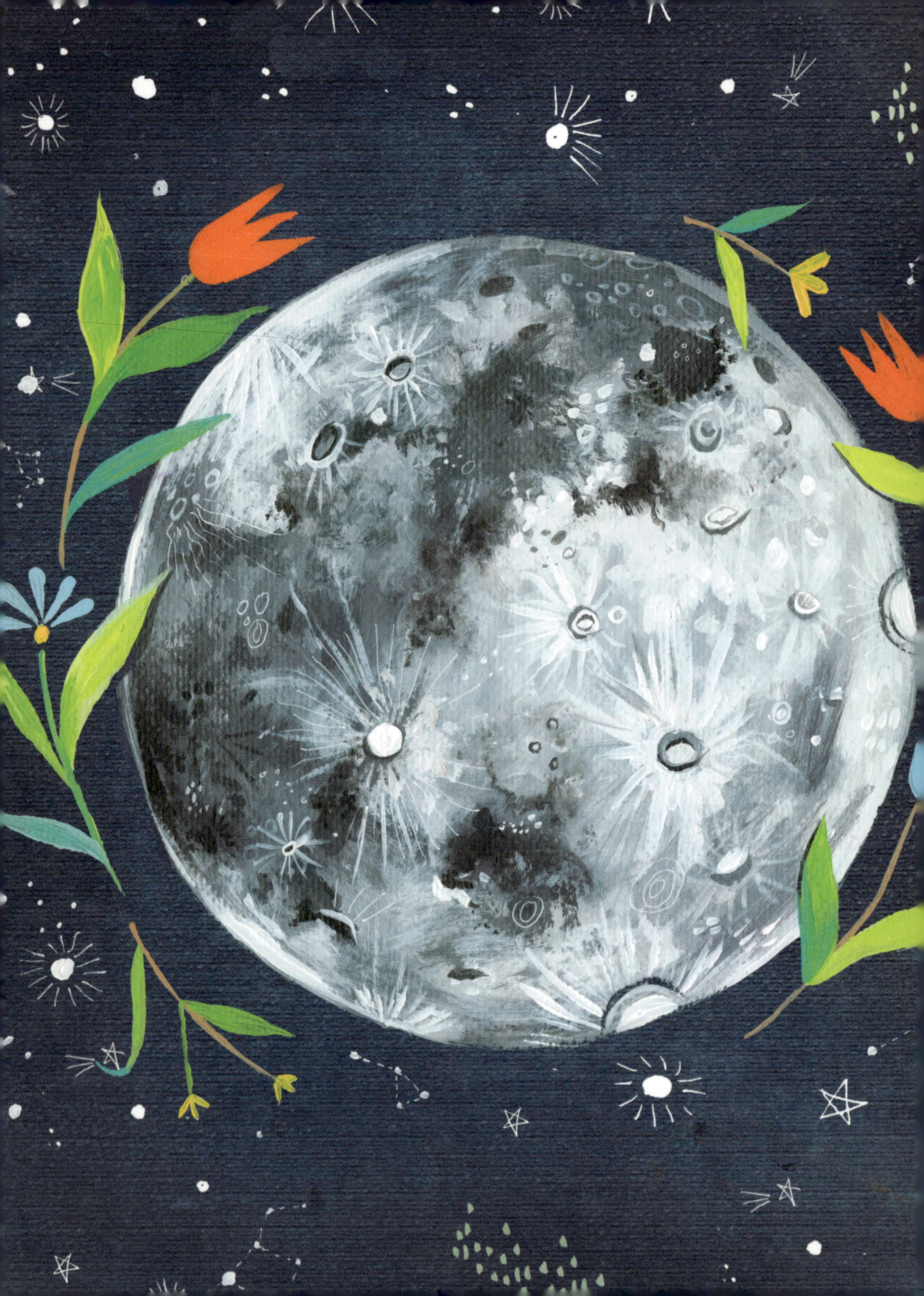

take a **FULL MOON HIKE**

let it light your path

Common Hazel

White Willow

Western Hemlock

European Larch

Wild Cherry

Coastal Redwood

Aspen

Sycamo[re]

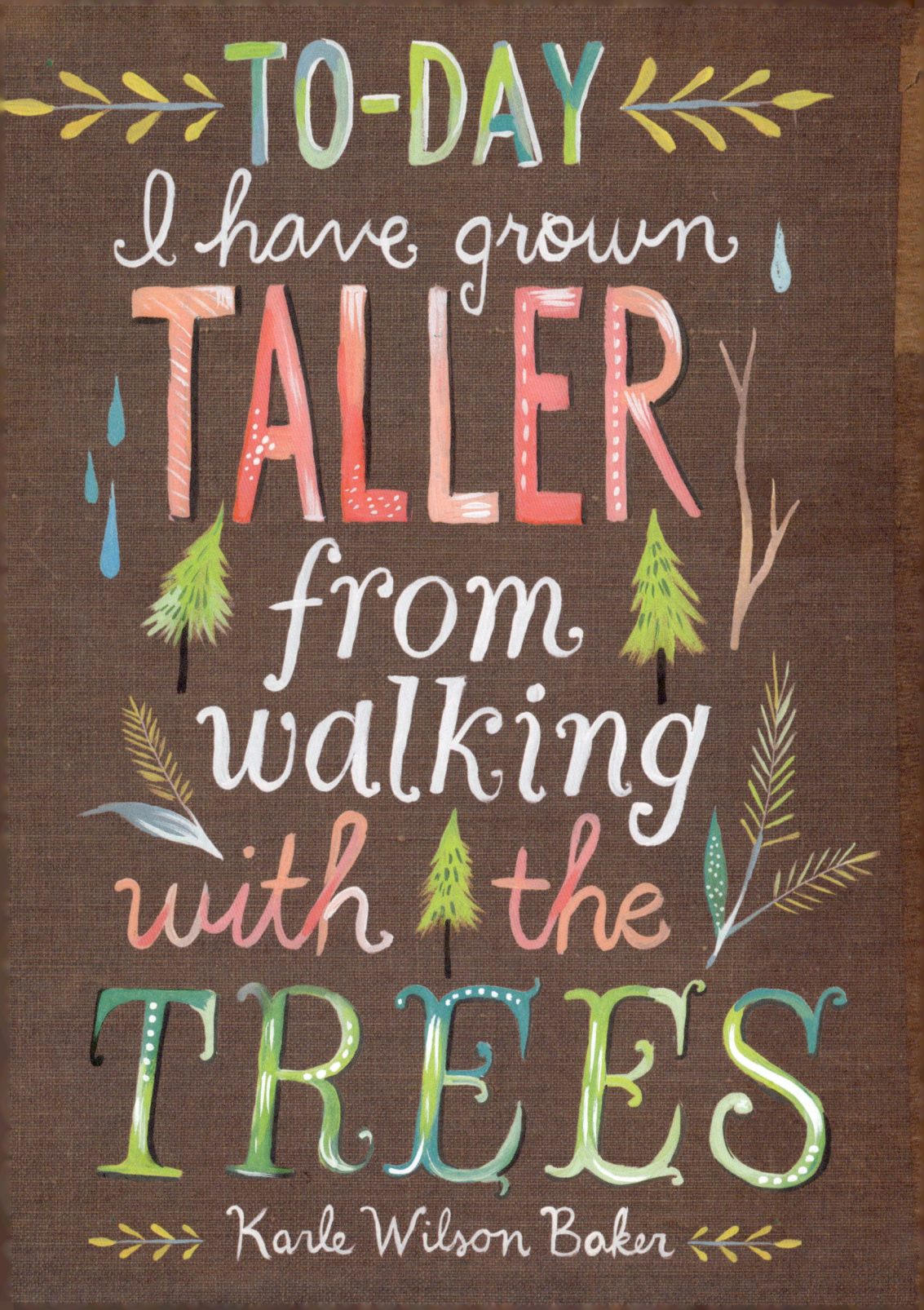

To-day I have grown TALLER from walking with the TREES

Karle Wilson Baker

TAKE A CANOE TRIP THAT CREEPS INTO THE NIGHT, THEN SET UP CAMP ON SHORE.

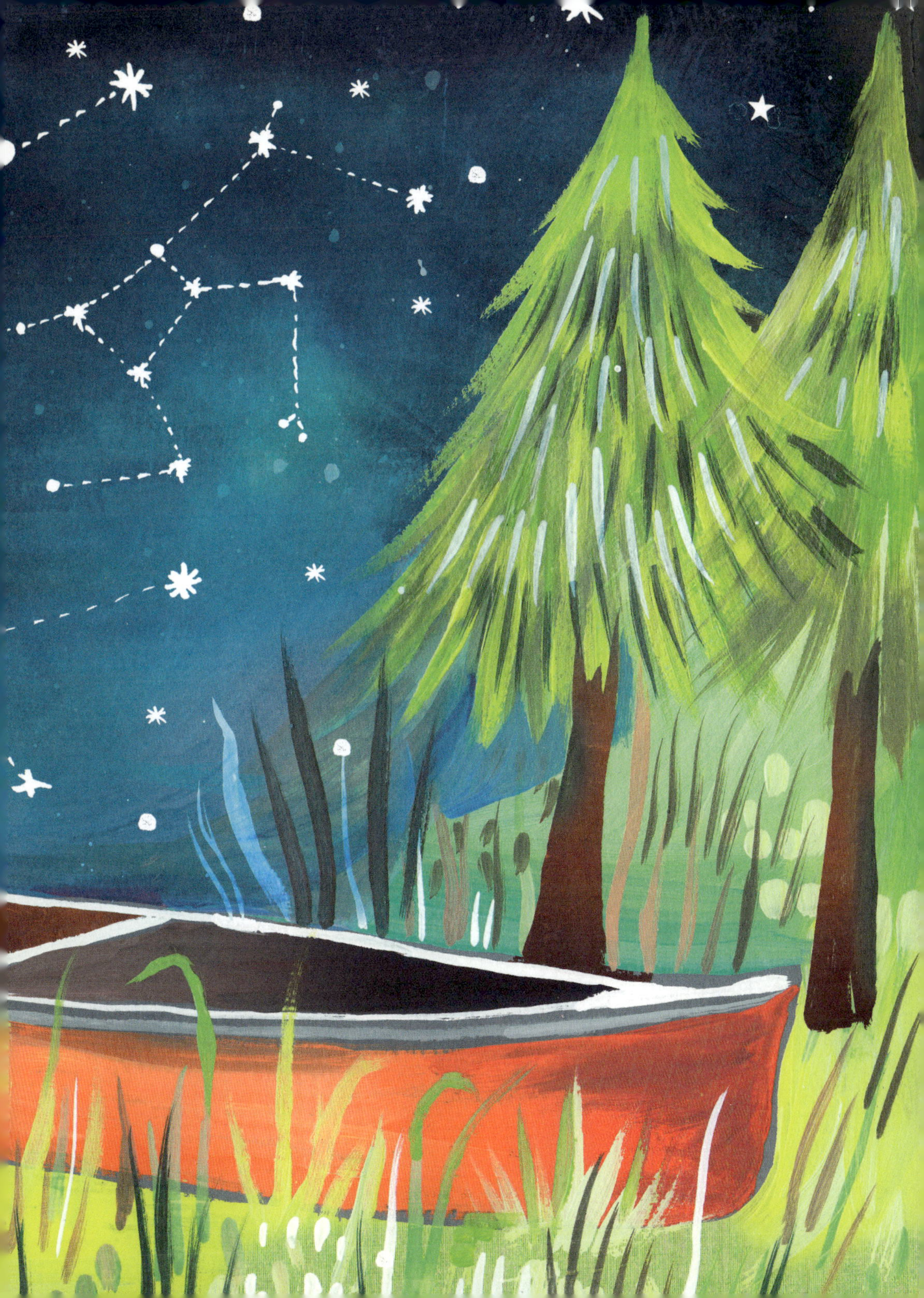

WHERE HAVE YOU BEEN?

WHERE ARE YOU GOING?

EAT

HER

FUNGI

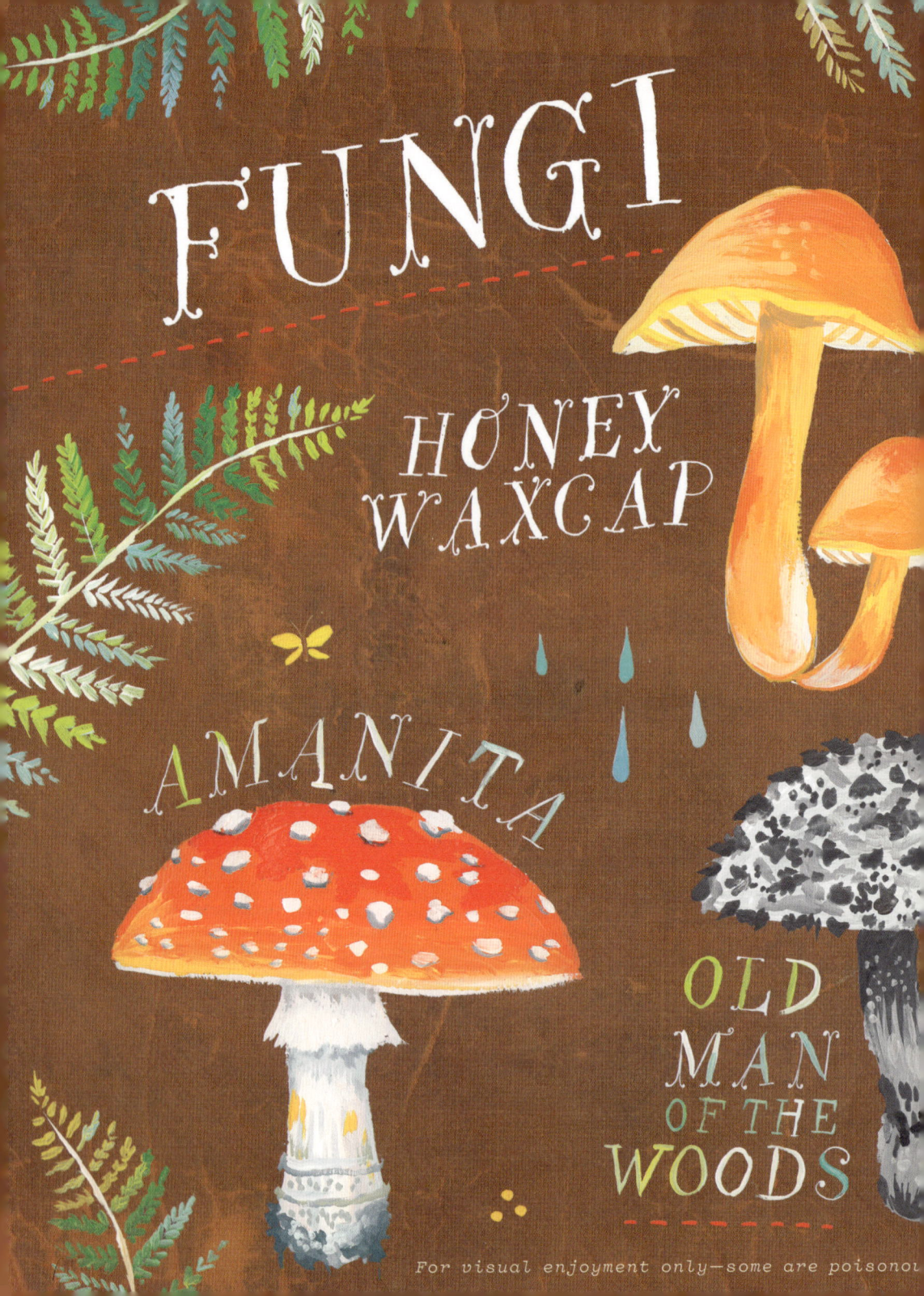

HONEY WAXCAP

AMANITA

OLD MAN OF THE WOODS

For visual enjoyment only—some are poisonou[s]

SHAGGY PARASOL

MOREL

CHANTERELLE

I must HAVE FLOWERS ALWAYS, ALWAYS.
—monet

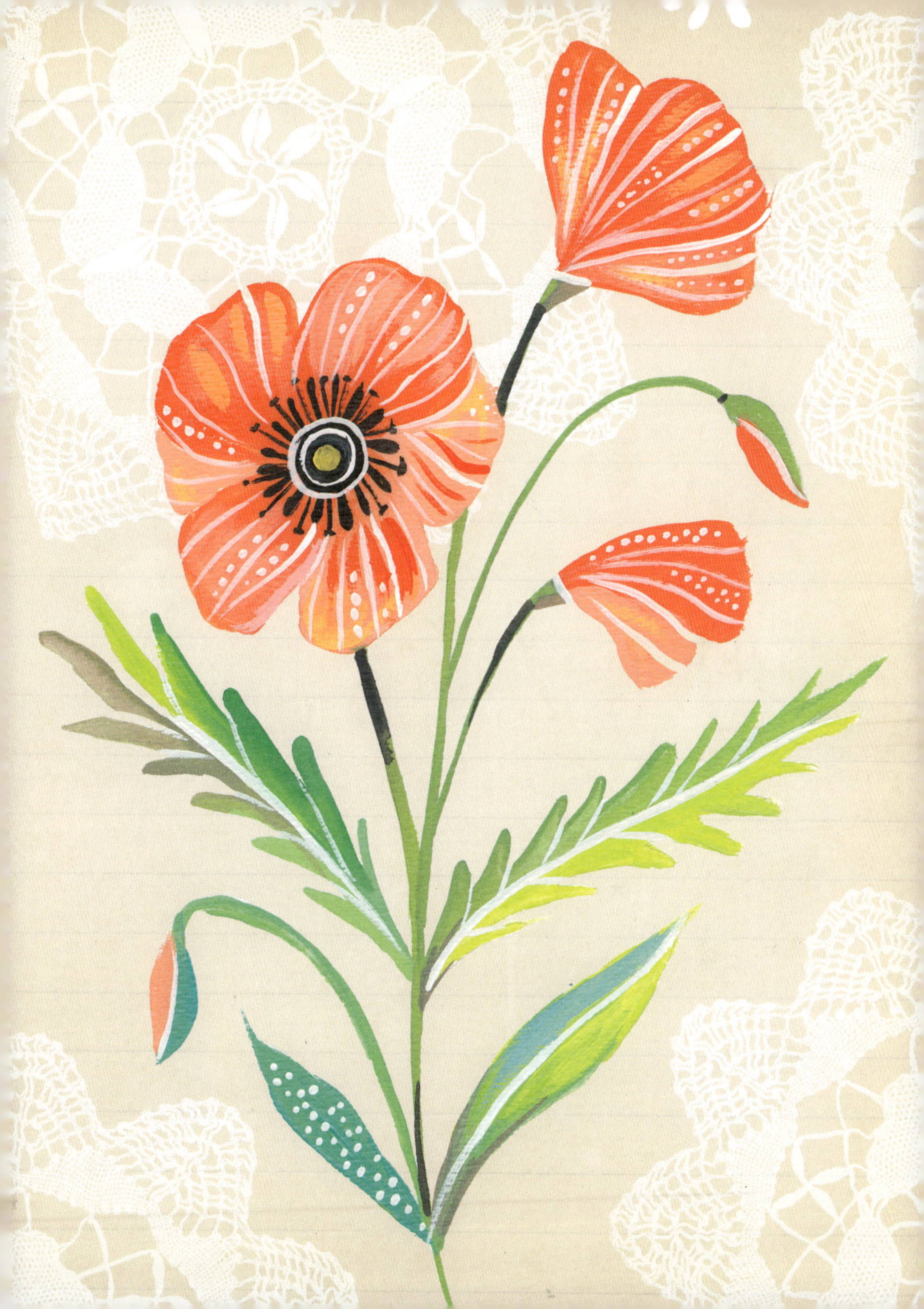

MOTHS

Io

Imperial

Luna

Cecropia

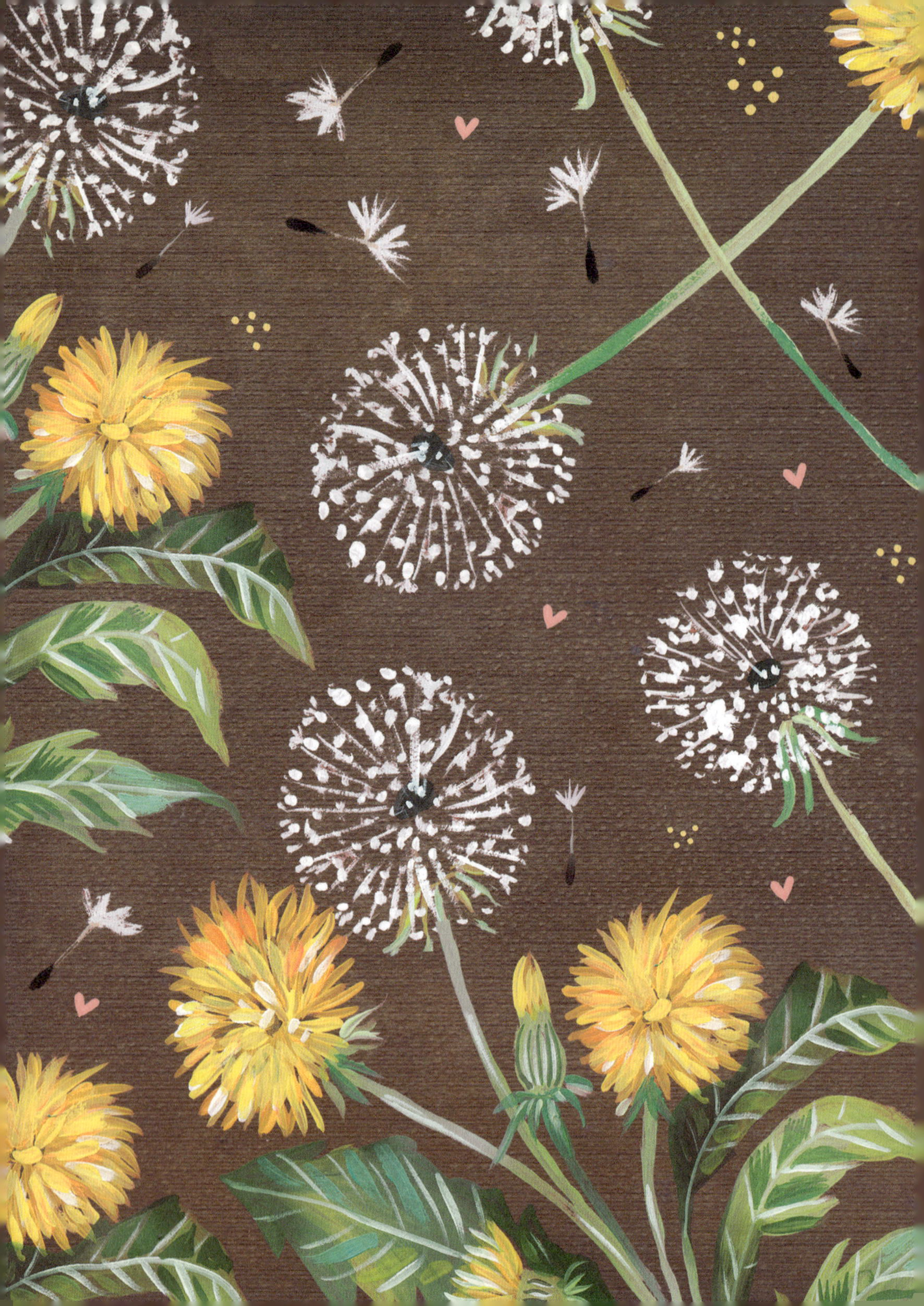

FIND A FIELD OF DANDELIONS. MAKE 100 WISHES.

Red-winged Blackbird

Oriole

Yellow Warbler

Purple Finch

Goldfinch

Bluejay

KNOW THESE BIRDS

grow a garden with cosmos, daisies, poppies & hummingbirds.

//
know these WILDFLOWERS

California Poppy

Cosmos

Black-eyed Susan

Wild Daisy

Purple Coneflower

Queen Anne's Lace

Buttercup

Bachelor's Button

press your

flowers here

cirrus

cirrostratus

altostratus

stratocumulus

cumulu

stratus

nimbostratu

cumulonimbus

cirrocumulus

altocumulus

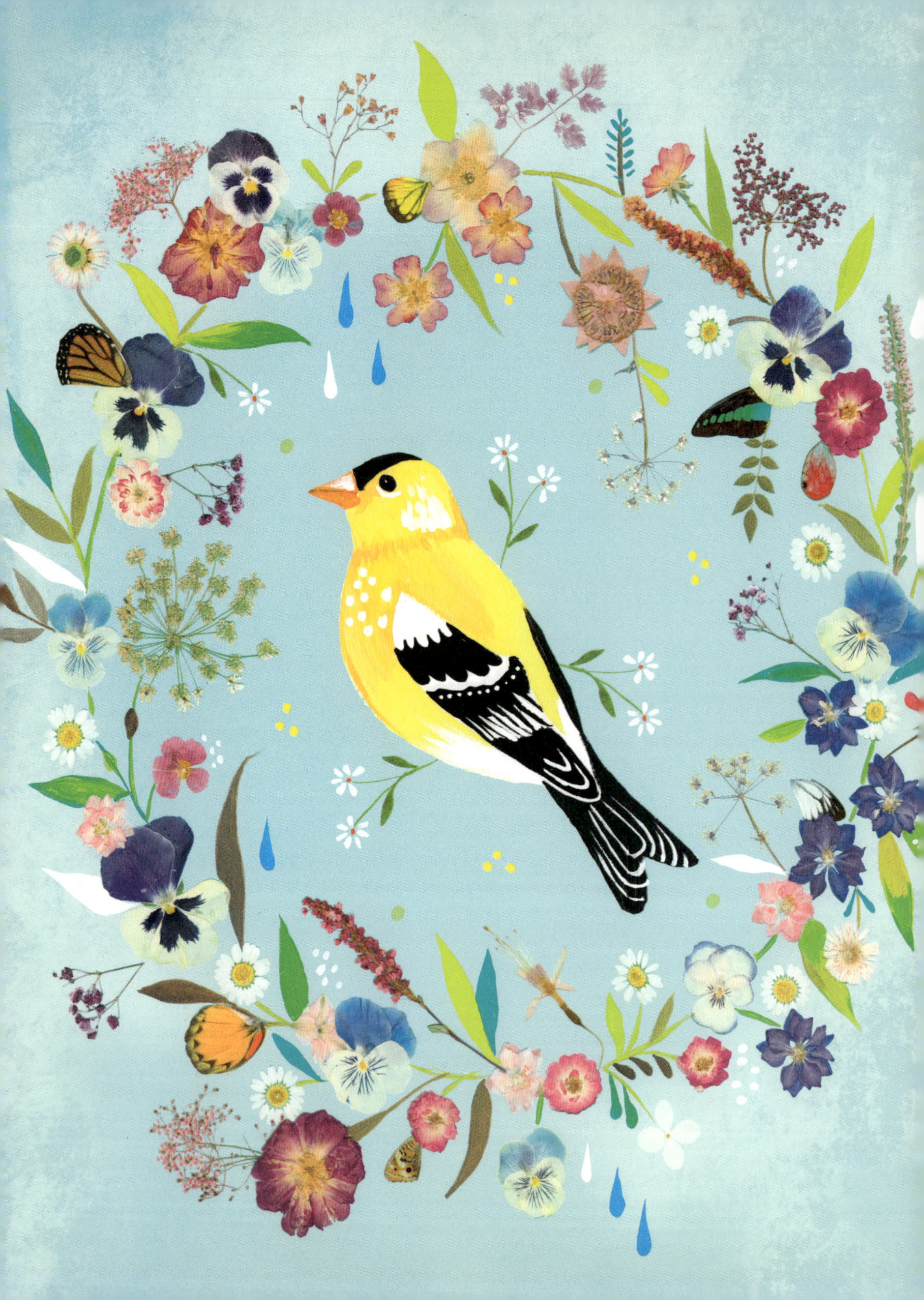

My Soul is made of meadow flowers

Gather:

A basketful of wildflowers and plants of various sizes. Be sure the stems are bendable.

Instructions:

1. Group flowers according to stem length.

2. Take the flowers with the shorter stems and put them in small bundles. Secure them by using one or two of the long-stemmed variety to tie the clusters together, as if using twine. Tie the knots gently so the stems don't break.

3. Finish enough bundles to create a circlet that, when the clusters overlap, sits nicely on the top of your head.

4. In the same manner as you secured the individual bundles, use the long-stemmed flowers to lash them all together.

This process can require a certain dexterity of the fingers and might be frustrating. Don't give up! Creativity often requires patience.

MAKE A WILDFLOWER CROWN

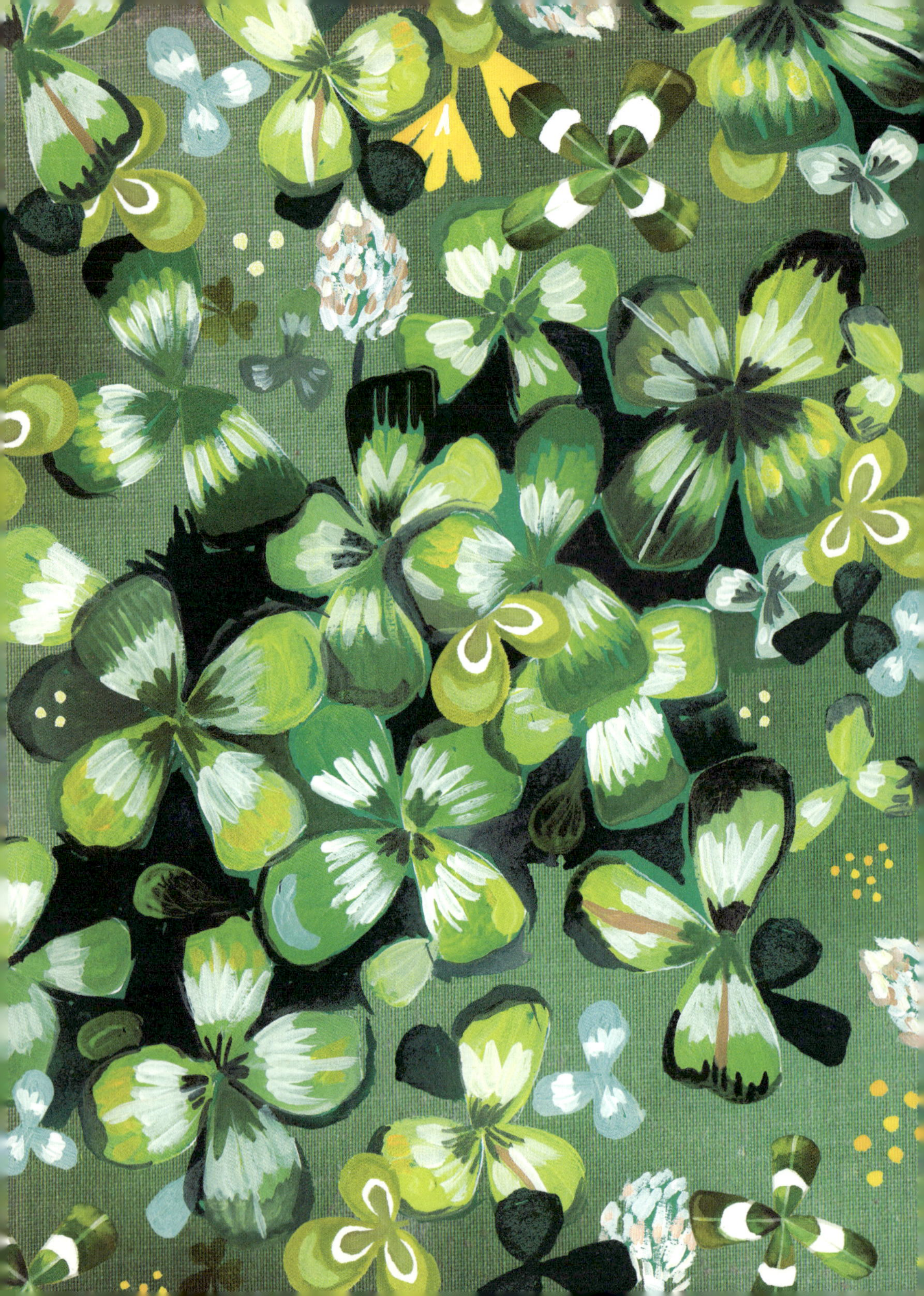

spend an hour looking for four-leaf clovers

press them in these pages

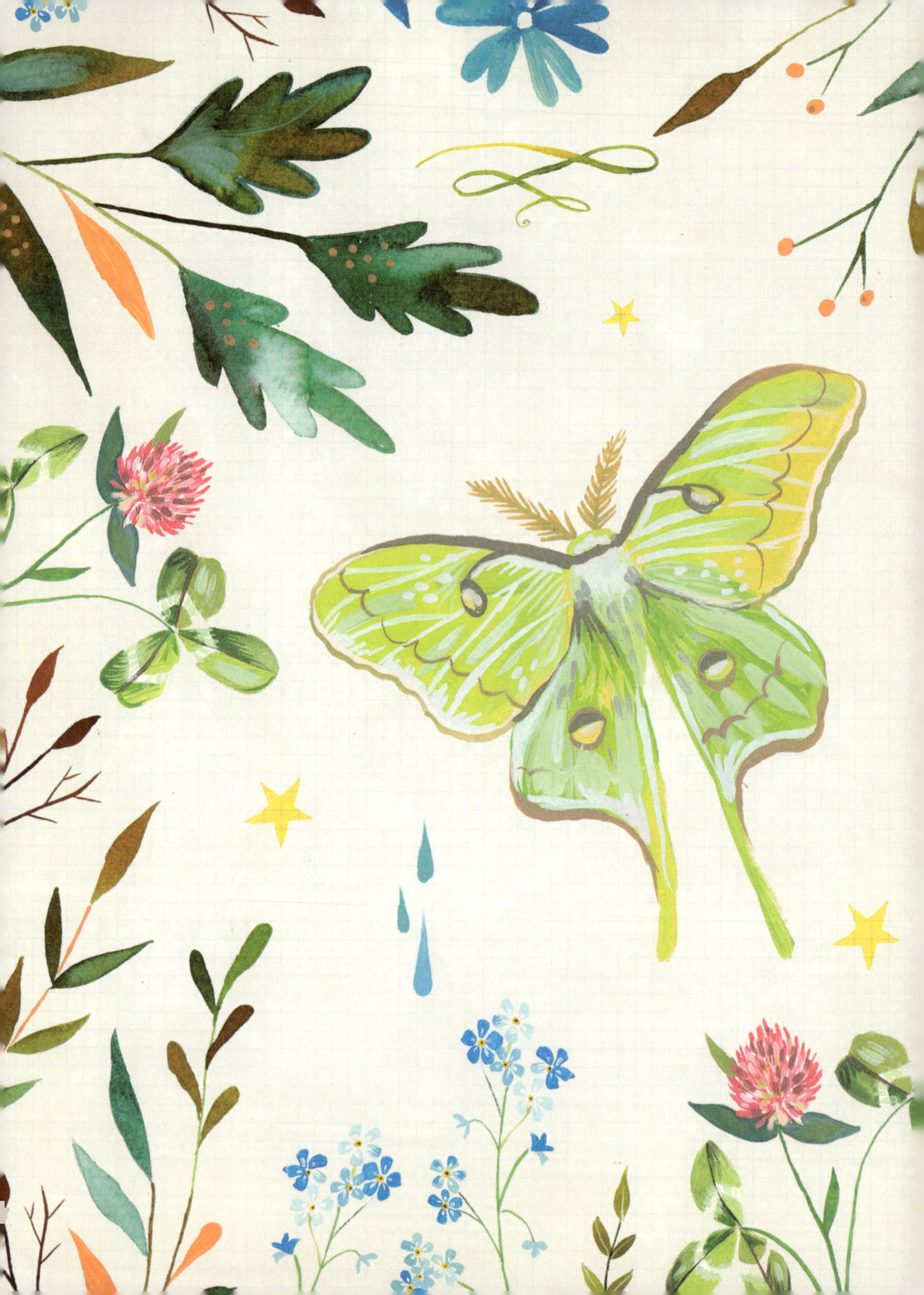

There is pleasure in
the pathless woods
There is a rapture
on the lonely shore
There is society
where none intrudes
By the deep sea,
and music in its roar
I love not man the
less but Nature more
—Lord Byron

KEEP BEES

Some Benefits of Keeping Bees:

- ♥ Honey
- ♥ Beeswax
- ♥ Connection to Nature
- ♥ Education
- ♥ The Best Pollinators

KEEP CHICKENS

Love and eggs are best when they are fresh.
— Russian Proverb

Explore a Tidepool

Octopus

Surfgrass

Mussel

Starfish

Sculpin

Anemone

Coral

Urchin

Crab

gather unlike frien

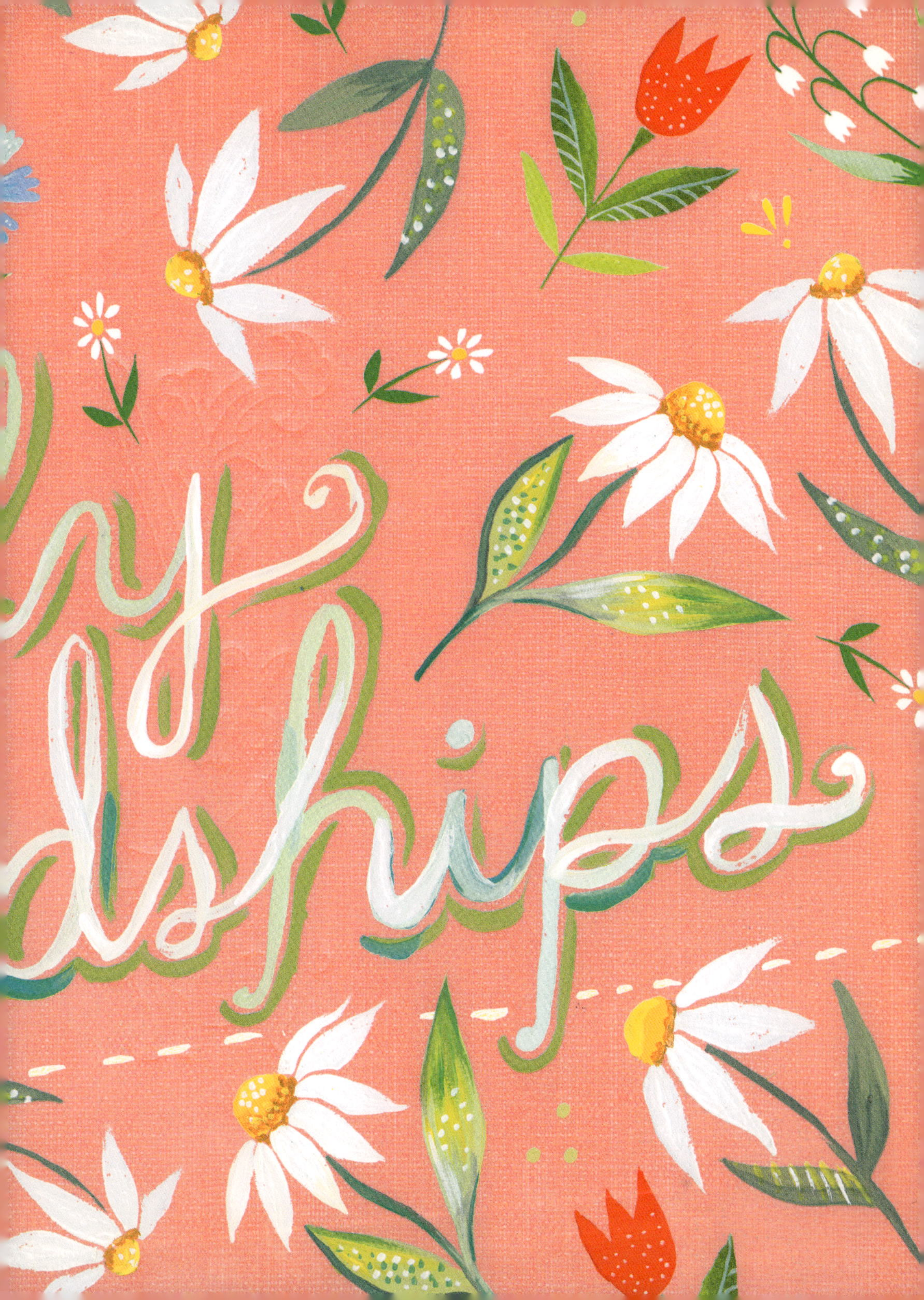
dships

SAY

YOR

lie in a lavender field

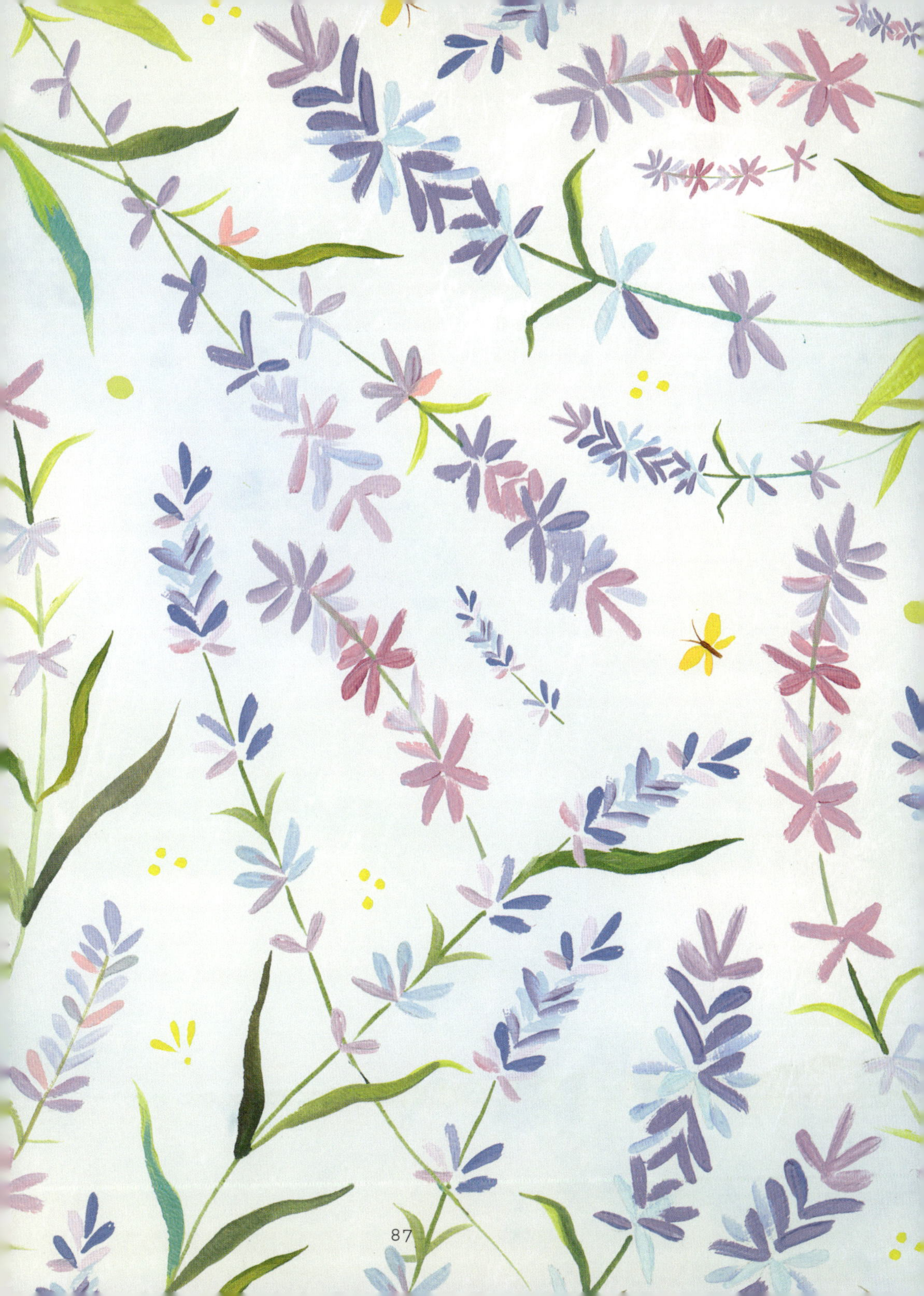

lavender simple syrup

Use this syrup in your summer cocktails, iced coffee, or lemonade!

1 cup (240 ml) pure water
2 cups (400 g) organic cane sugar
4 Tbsp (60 g) fresh lavender

Heat the water until boiling and add the cane sugar.

Simmer for 20 minutes, stirring often, until the sugar dissolves. Turn off the heat but do not remove from the stove top.

Remove the petals from the lavender, discarding the stems.

While the syrup is still hot, crush the lavender in the palms of your hands and add petals to the liquid.

Cover and let stand for an additional 10 minutes or longer to draw the lavender flavors into the syrup.

Use a muslin cloth to strain the lavender buds out of syrup, and pour directly into a glass bottle or jar.

Cover and refrigerate to extend the life of the syrup.

EAT BERRIES STRAIGHT FROM THE VINE

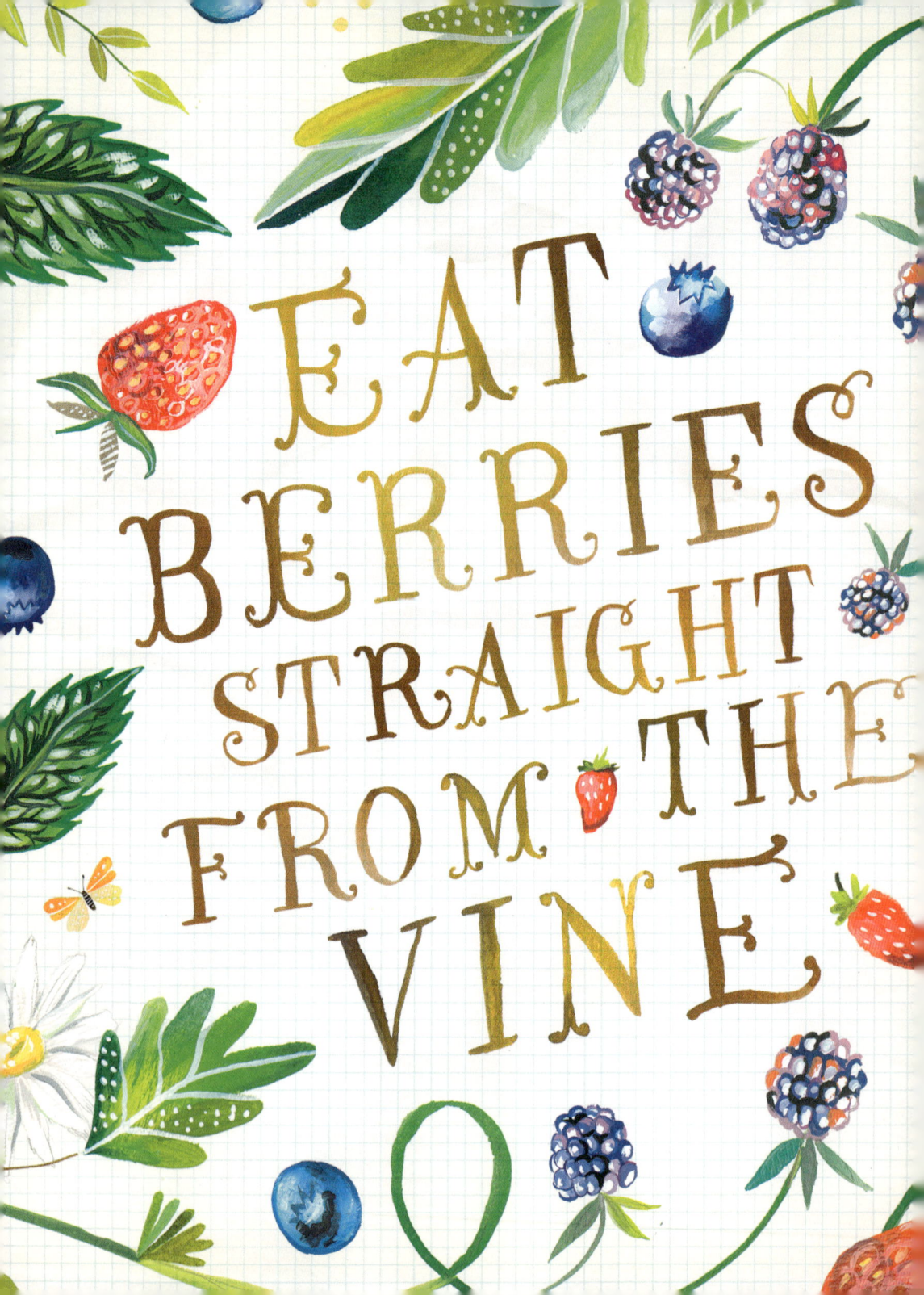

ROBIN — CHEERILY-CHEERILY-CHEER-UP!

CARDINAL — BIRDIE-BIRDIE-BIRDIE

EASTERN TOWHEE

Learn to identify birdsongs

CHICKA-DEE-DEE-DEE-DEE!
CHICKADEE
DRINK-YOUR-TEEEE!
TURR-TURLEE-TURLEE!
EASTERN BLUEBIRD

WALK DOWN A DIRT PATH AT SUNSET

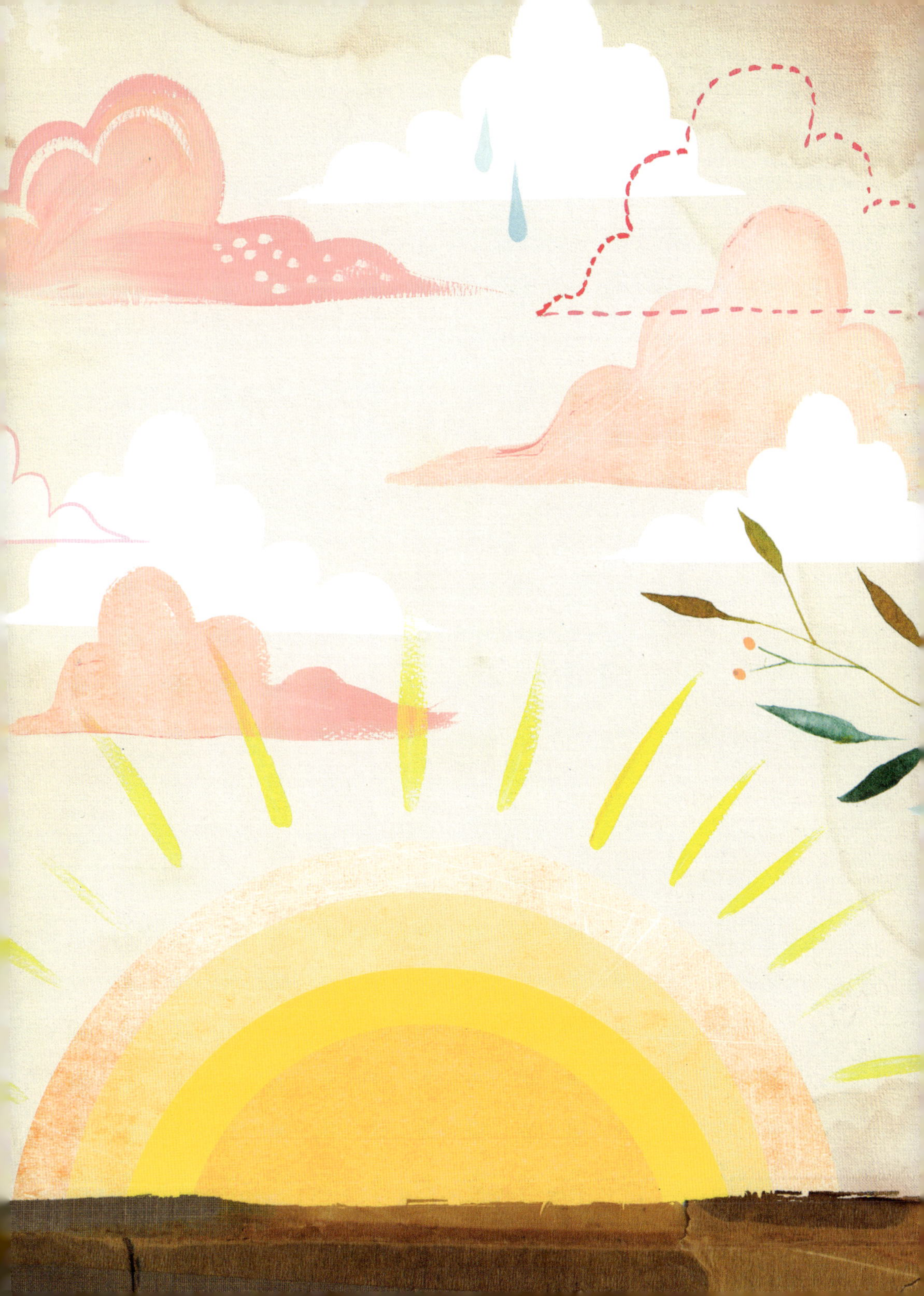

see the Northern Lights

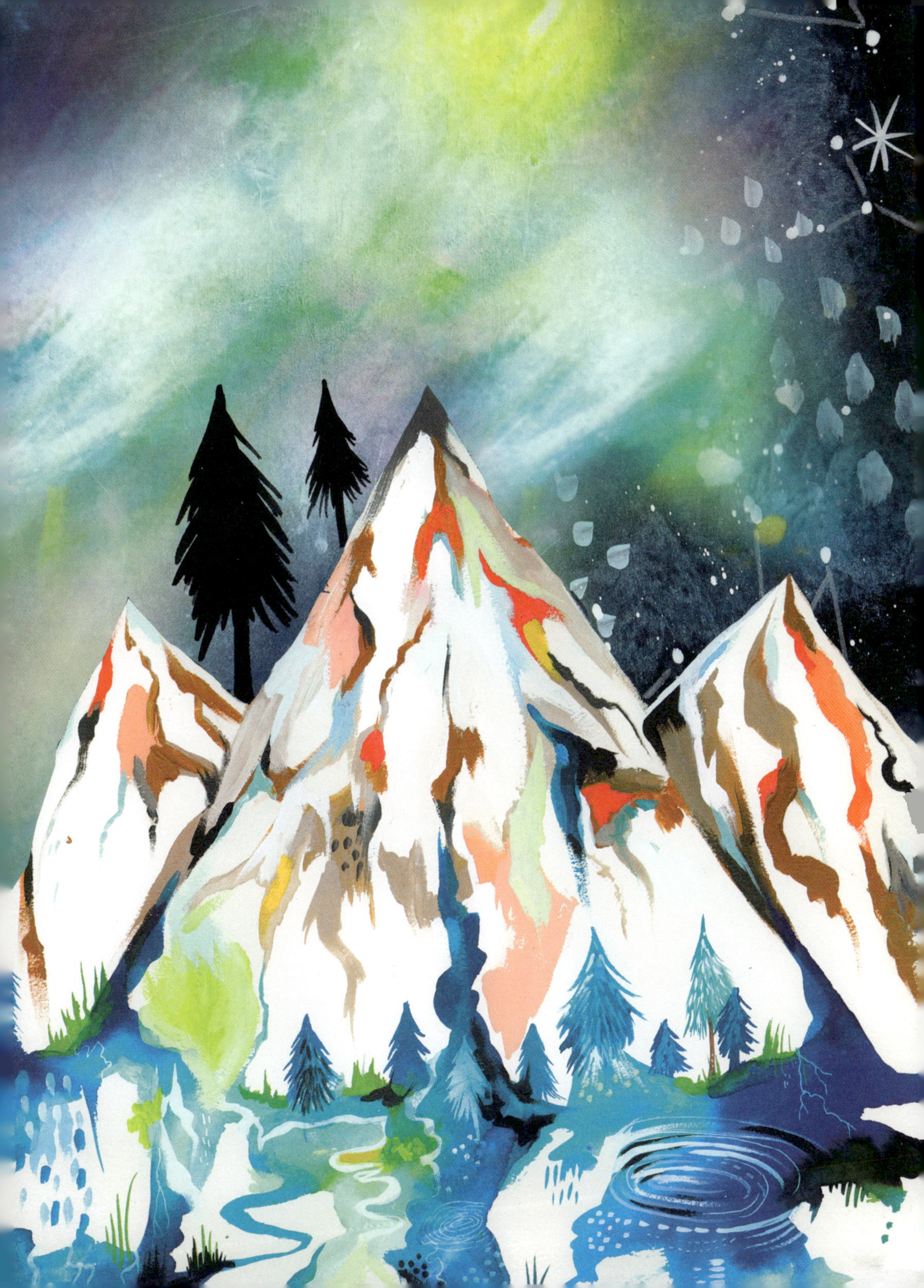

BACK FLOAT in a SUN-WARMED LAKE

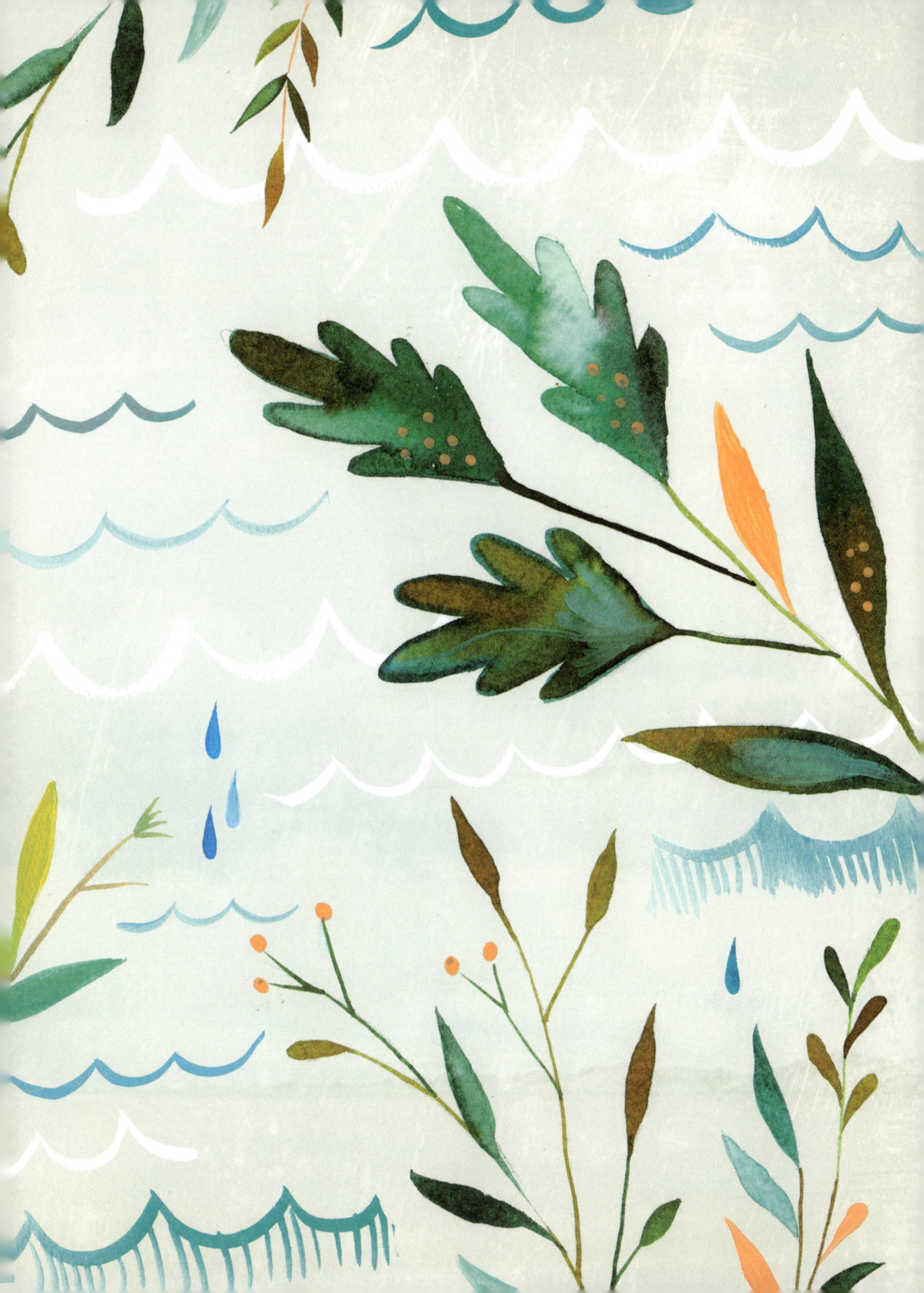

Take a SUMMER MINERAL BATH with the windows open

2 cups (480 ml) milk or buttermilk
1 cup (240 ml) honey
1 cup (270 g) pink Himalayan salt
A handful or two of fresh or dried rose petals & buds
A handful of fresh or dried chamomile flowers

Pour the milk, honey, and salt into warm running bathwater. Swirl the water around to mix everything well. When the tub is full, sprinkle in the roses and chamomile flowers. Sink in, exhale, and soak for 15 to 30 minutes. This bath will leave your skin feeling soft and smooth, detoxify your body, and invite peace and relaxation.

She smelled of sun and daisies with a hint of river water

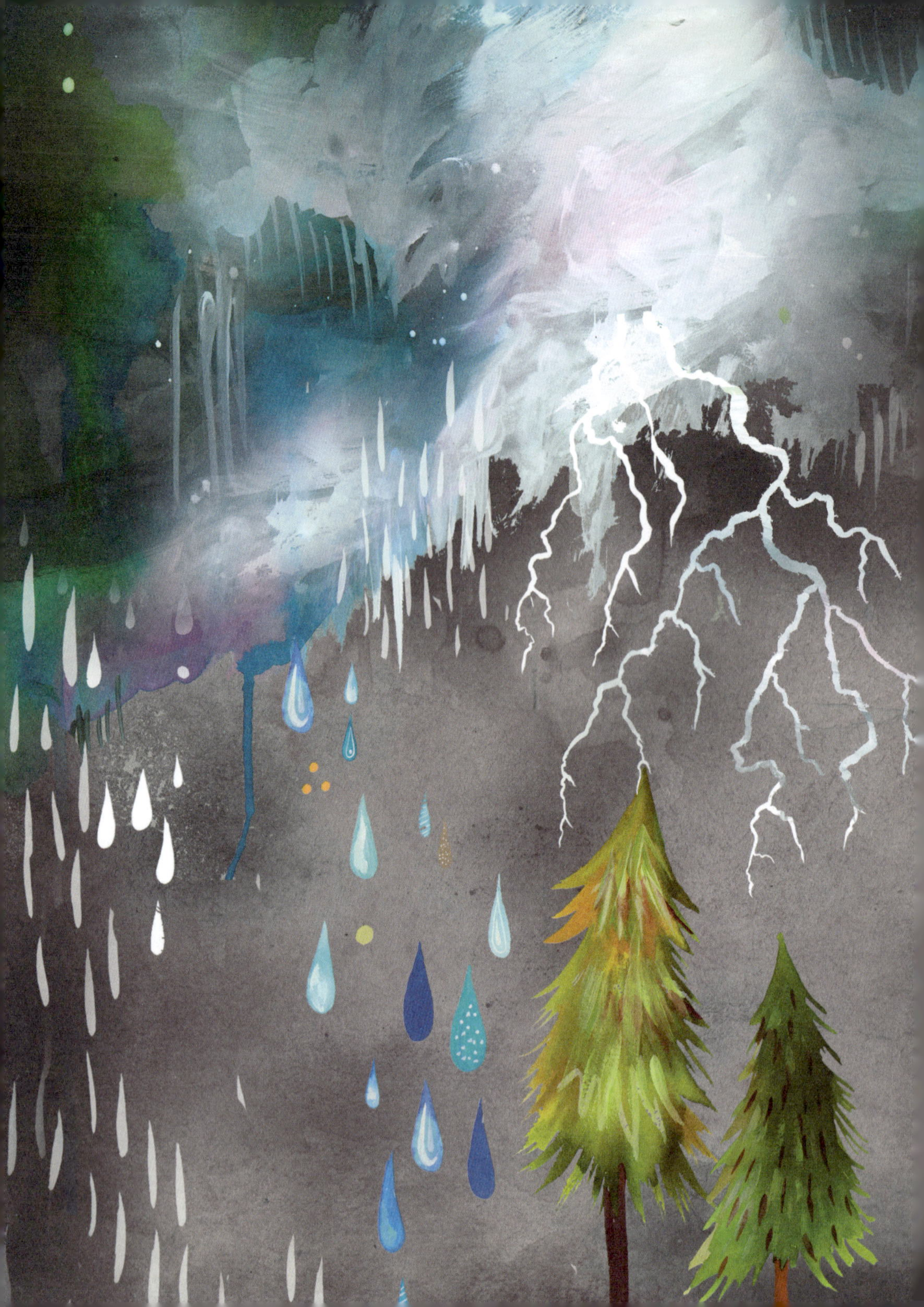

fall asleep during a wild summer thunderstorm

Cover Me in L

lilacs

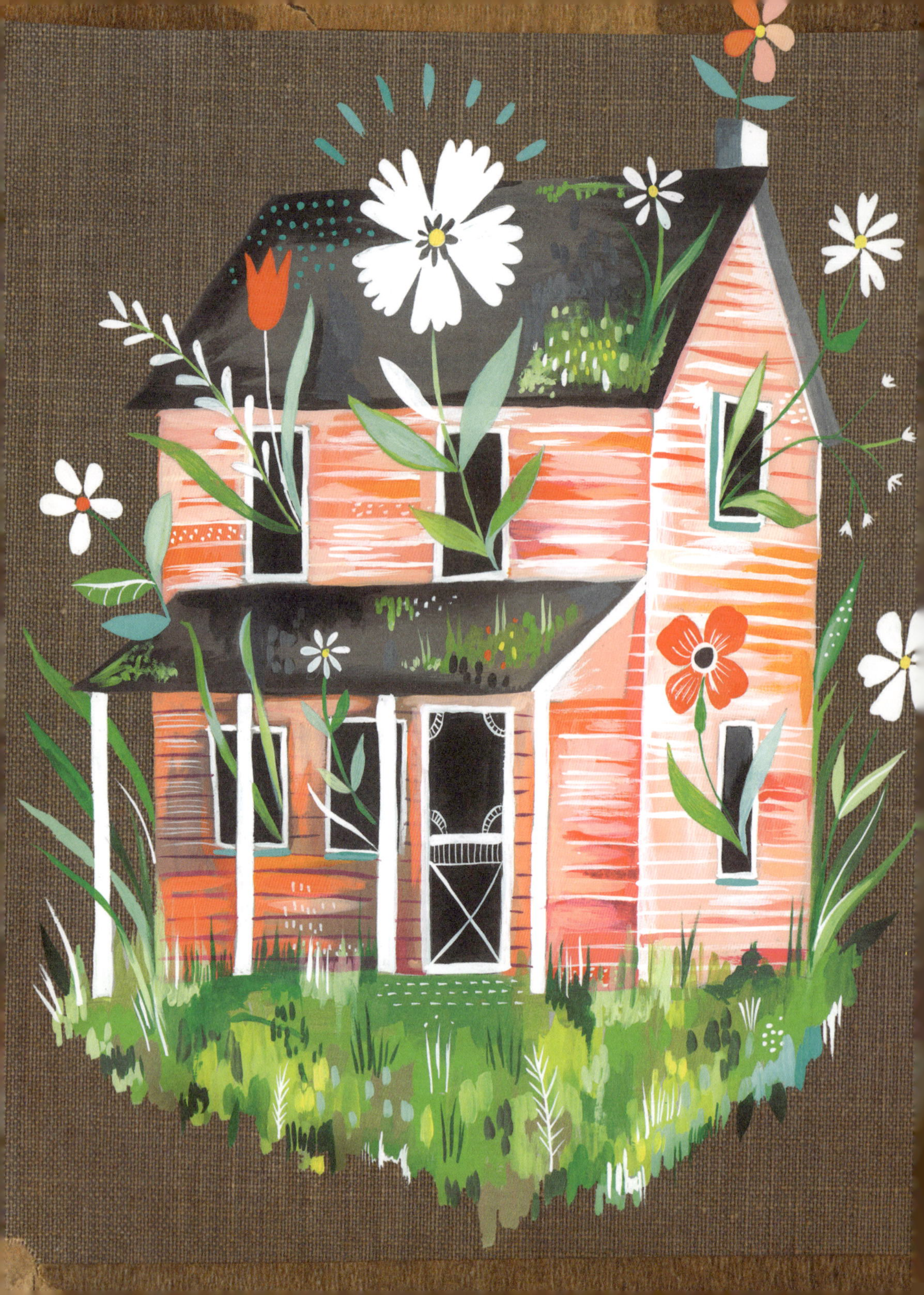

hang your clothes on the line. they'll be infused with sun & breeze & birdsong stumble upon a farm stand in the middle of nowhere

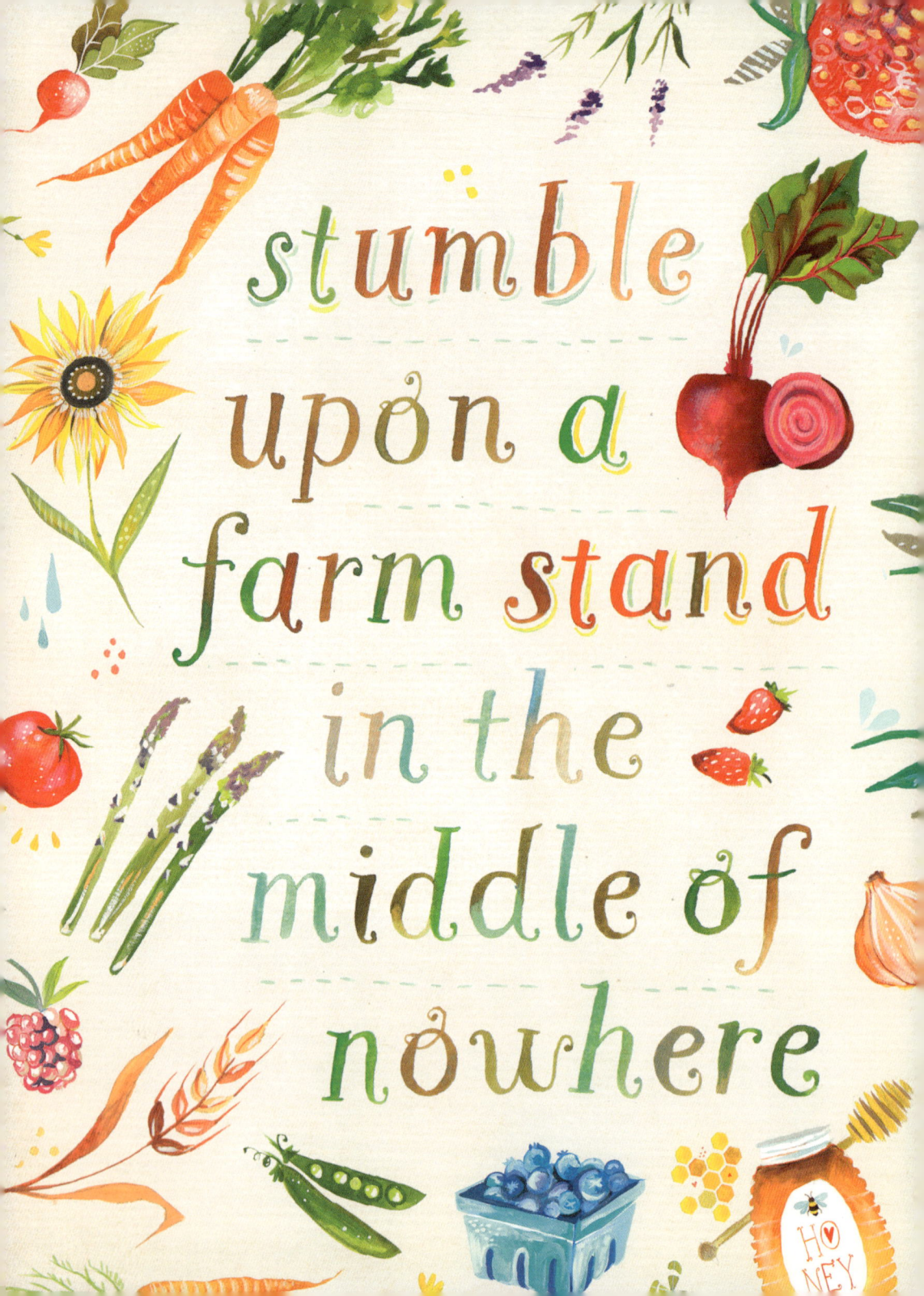

Make a STRAWBERRY PIE from scratch

CRUST

- 2½ cups (300 g) organic, all-purpose flour
- 1 Tbsp organic cane sugar
- 1 tsp salt
- 1 cup (220 g) unsalted butter, cubed & chilled
- ½ cup (120 ml) very cold water

Blend the flour, sugar, and salt together in a large bowl. Use your fingertips to work the butter into the mixture until the largest pieces of butter are slightly bigger than your thumbnail. Pour in the water and mix with a wooden spoon or spatula until the dough becomes a single mass, then knead with your hands several times and form into a ball. Divide the dough into two equal parts, wrap each portion in plastic wrap, and chill for at least one hour.

FILLING

2 cups (400 g) fresh strawberries
½ cup (120 ml) water
½ cup (100 g) organic cane sugar
Juice of 1 lemon
Handful of fresh basil leaves, minced
Pinch of freshly ground cinnamon

ASSEMBLE & BAKE

Thoroughly wash the strawberries and cut half of them into thumbnail sized pieces. Place in a pan over medium heat with a very small splash of water, then pour the sugar over the strawberries and cover. Stir occasionally, adding small amounts of water and lemon juice to keep from sticking to the pan. Once the strawberries have cooked down and their juices begin to thicken, add the basil and remove from the heat. Keep covered.

Cut the remaining strawberries in half and place them in a small bowl. Add the cinnamon, and shake.

Remove the chilled dough and roll each part out on a floured surface until it's about ¼ inch (6 mm) thick. Place one disk into a 9-inch (23 cm) pie pan, then gently press into the bottom of the pan without tearing the dough. Place the halved strawberries into your crust, then pour the strawberry mixture from the pan over them. Cover with the second piece of dough and crimp the edges all around the pie pan so that it forms a bond with the bottom crust. Make four symmetrical cuts in the top, in any pattern you choose, which will allow the pie to vent while baking. Place on the center rack in the oven and cook at 450°F (230°C) for about 12 minutes or until the crust turns golden brown around the edges. Remove and allow to cool slightly before cutting. Serve hot or refrigerate for at least 30 minutes to serve chilled.

GO ON A TREK FOR WILD MAINE BLUEBERRIES

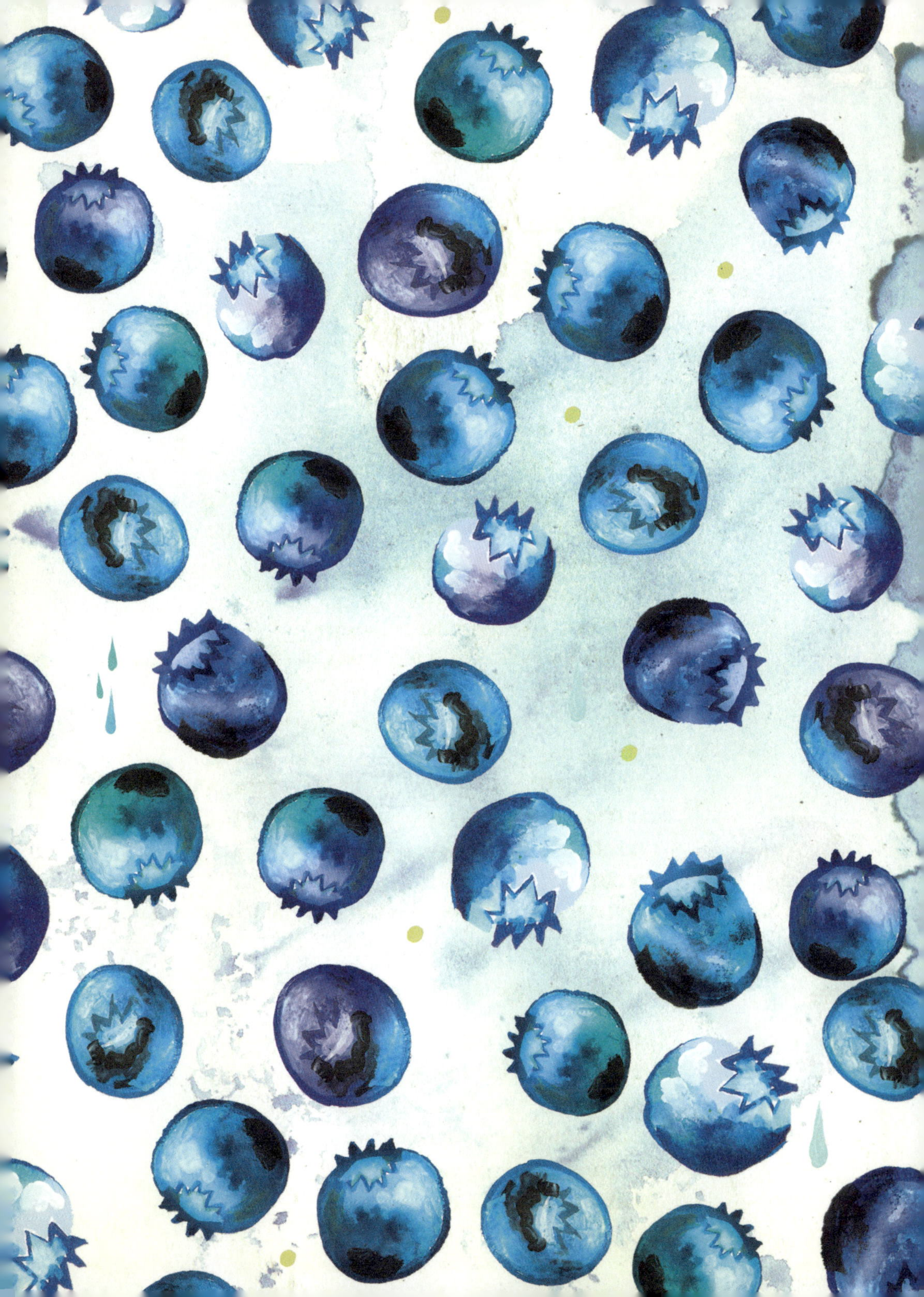

GIVE ME THE splendid SILENT SUN

with all his BEAMS FULL dazzling

—walt whitman

Sa
BEA

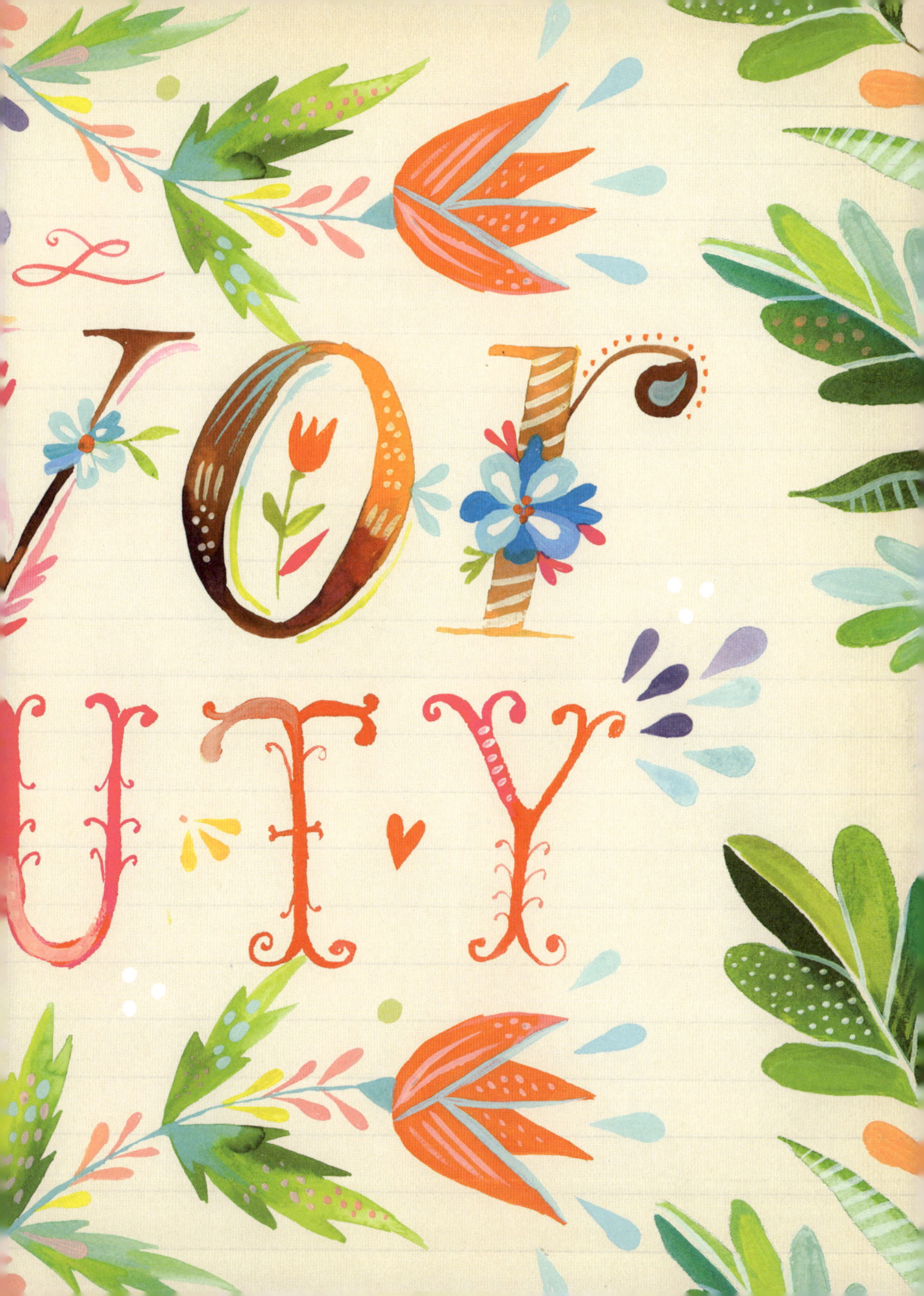
vor
UTY

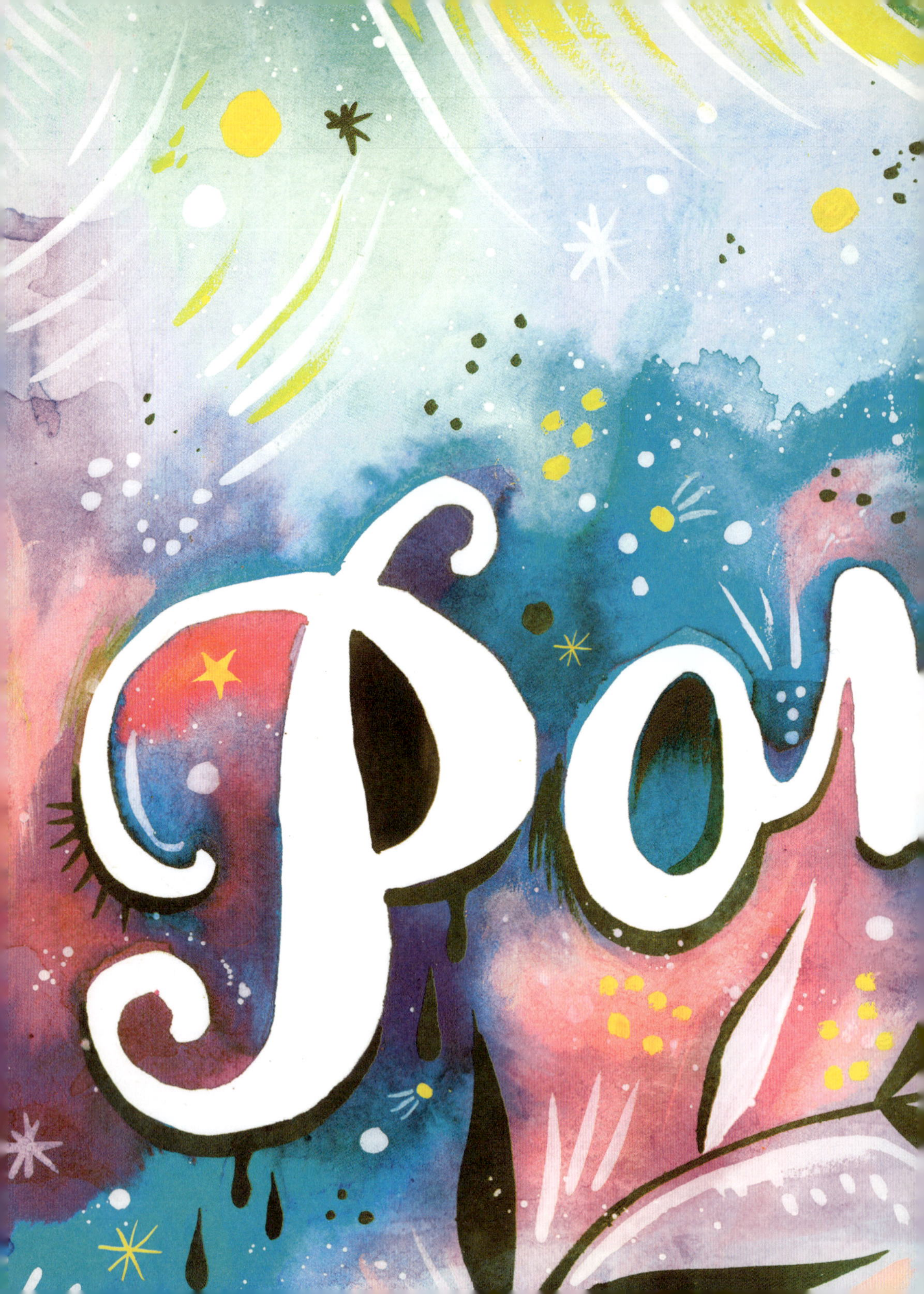
Po

der

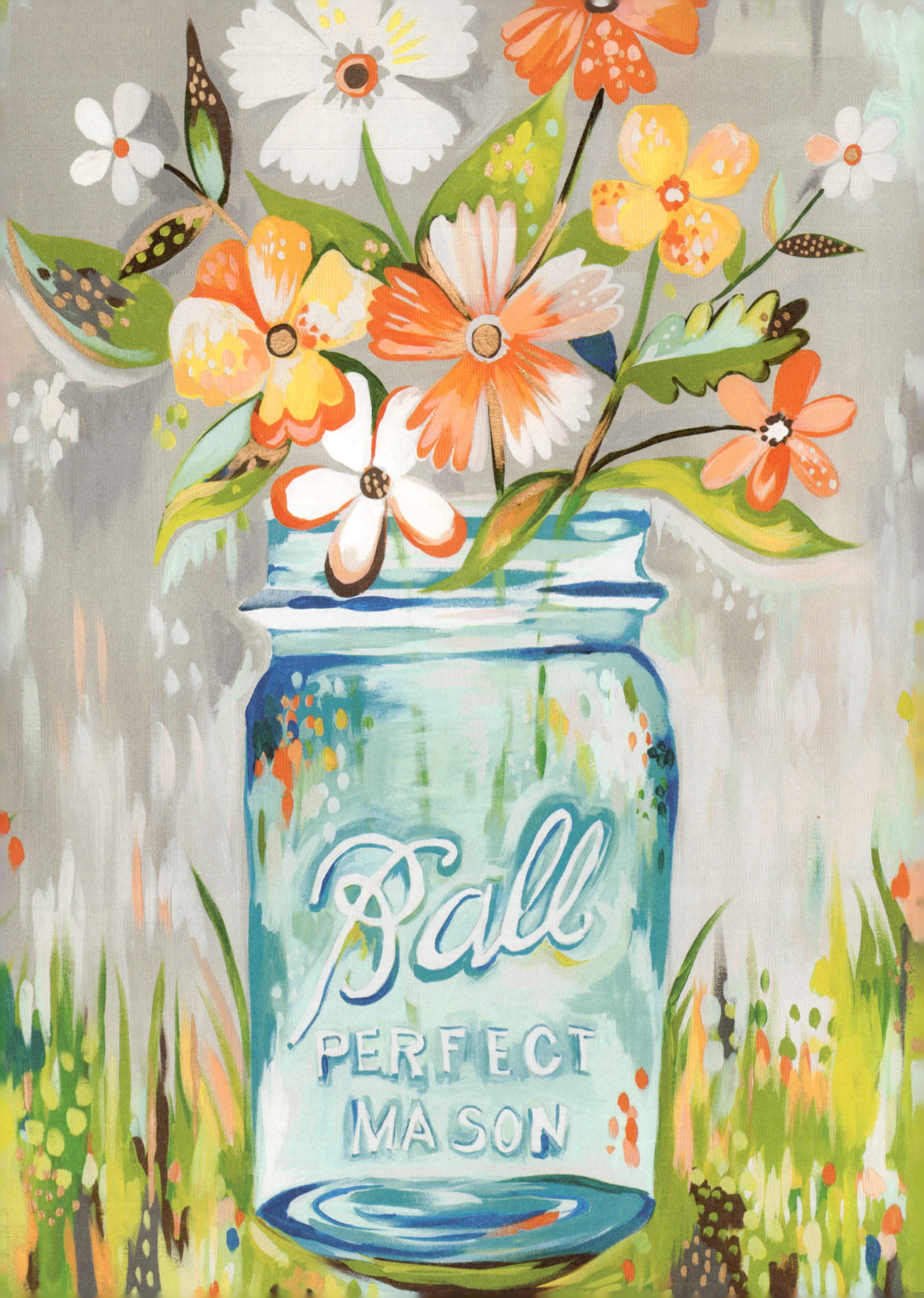
Ball
PERFECT
MASON

HOW TO EVOKE A DAYDREAM

Gather three or more of the following items:

    a cup of tea
    a journal
    fresh cut flowers
    a rainstorm
    old photographs
    your favorite book
    a wishing dandelion
    a crystal

1. Find a quiet spot (in a sunny meadow or in the shade of a tree).

2. Take several deep breaths to sink into the moment.

3. Gaze at your items for several minutes.

4. Close your eyes and drift away into a pleasant thought (a faraway place, a creative idea, a sweet memory).

5. Take another deep breath.

6. Stay awhile.

Make a NATURE MANDALA

The mandala originates in Eastern traditions dating back thousands of years. It is often created with intricate patterns of colored sand over the course of many days of meditation and ceremony. At the completion of the ritual, all the sand and colors of the painting are gathered together and poured into a body of flowing water. In this way, the mandala represents the impermanence of life and the fluid nature of the universe.

Create your own symbol of beauty and impermanence by using objects found in nature. Take a basket into the garden or forest. Gather many items that speak to your spirit (leaves, pinecones, seeds, flower petals, stones). Remember to be gentle on the earth—pick only what you need.

Find a location to create your mandala. A flat section of ground or beach works well. Start by putting one item down. This will be the center of your mandala. Encircle that item with other natural materials, as pictured. You may alternate the pattern by material, color, or shape. Continue this process until you reach a desired size.

Be still for a while with the art you've just created. After meditating on the mandala for a good while, destroy it! Scatter the petals in the air or throw the materials into the river.

Ursa Major

Cassiopeia

know these
CONSTE[

Hercules

ATIONS

Cancer

Orion

Keep these CRYSTALS nearby for their POWERS and PROTECTIONS:

BLACK TOURMALINE

Reduces stress, protects from negative forces & energy. An electric, grounding stone.

LABRADORITE

A magical stone. Awakens your psychic abilities, enhancing your intuition and awareness. Protects your aura from negativity.

ROSE QUARTZ

Stone of love (all types) - self love, family love, erotic love. Use to raise self-esteem & balance emotions. A peaceful, calming crystal.

CITRINE

Stone of abundance and manifestation. Expands imagination, creativity, and personal power.

TIGER'S EYE

A balancing stone. Protects during adventures. Brings wealth and prosperity.

FLUORITE

Absorbs negative energy. Opens the third eye. Protects on a psychic level and aids in stabilization. A meditative stone.

AMETHYST

Stone of the spirit. Peaceful, calming crystal. Sets mind and emotions at ease. Aids in overcoming addiction.

SPIRIT ANIMALS

hummingbird

Throughout many ancient cultures, animal totems have been an important part of our connection to nature and finding our place in the world. Just as every person is unique, each spirit animal has different qualities, strengths, and personality characteristics.

fox — cleverness, quick wit, luck, charm, mischievousness

playfulness, intelligence, quirkiness, creativity

horse — wanderlust, freedom, grace, guidance, endurance

joy, love, magic, hope

strength, bravery, confidence, power

bear

Coming to know your spirit animal can be a profound experience. To begin this journey, spend time alone among the creatures in nature.

otter

Keep a journal, taking note of animal appearances in dreams and works of art, and reflect upon your own unique qualities. The ancients believed that your animal finds you! Keep watch and listen closely.

whale

wisdom, peace, gentleness, depth of emotion

HOW TO BE STILL

Stand tall like a tree.

Plant your feet into the earth.

Sigh out loud.

Listen to the world that surrounds you.

Become one with your breath.

Watch your thoughts come & go like clouds floating by.

Sink into the present moment.

Just be.

Stand in the middle of an open meadow or field.

Close your eyes and take a deep breath.

Open your eyes to the sky, stretch your arms wide, and exclaim

"I AM ALIVE!"

Don't worry, the prairie will never judge you and the wildflowers will stand in reverence of your bravery.

There shall be an eternal summer in the grateful heart

—celia thaxter

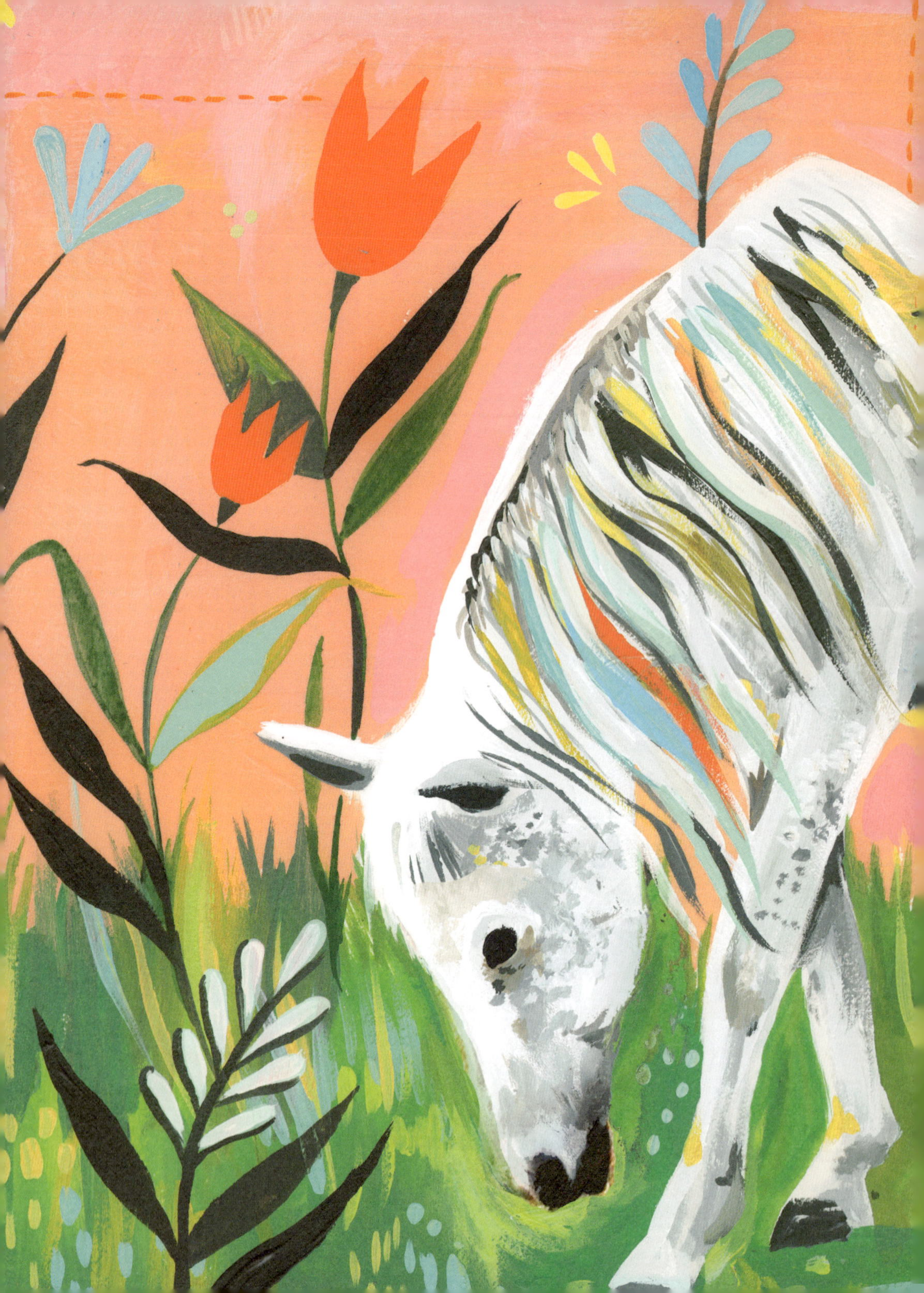

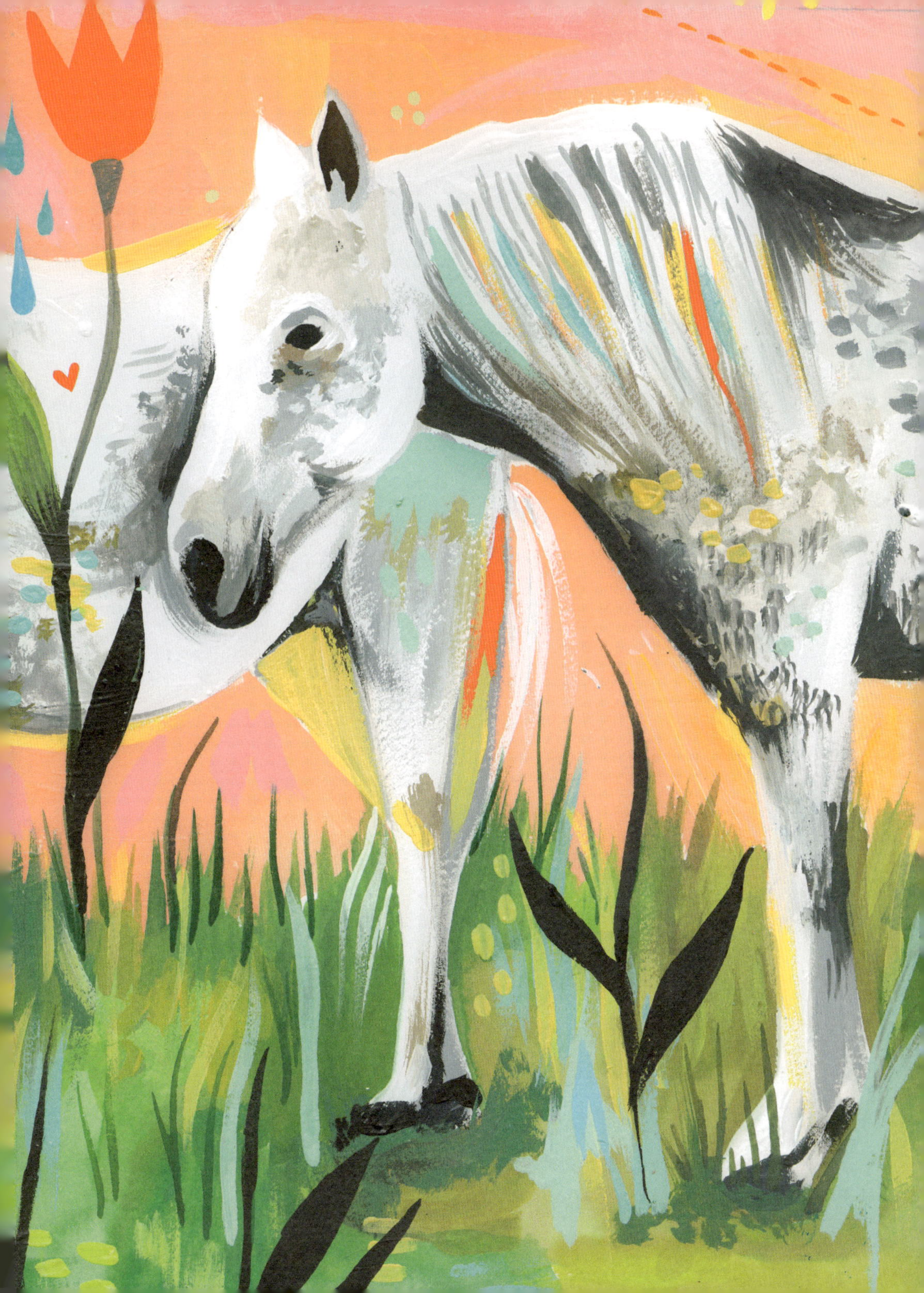

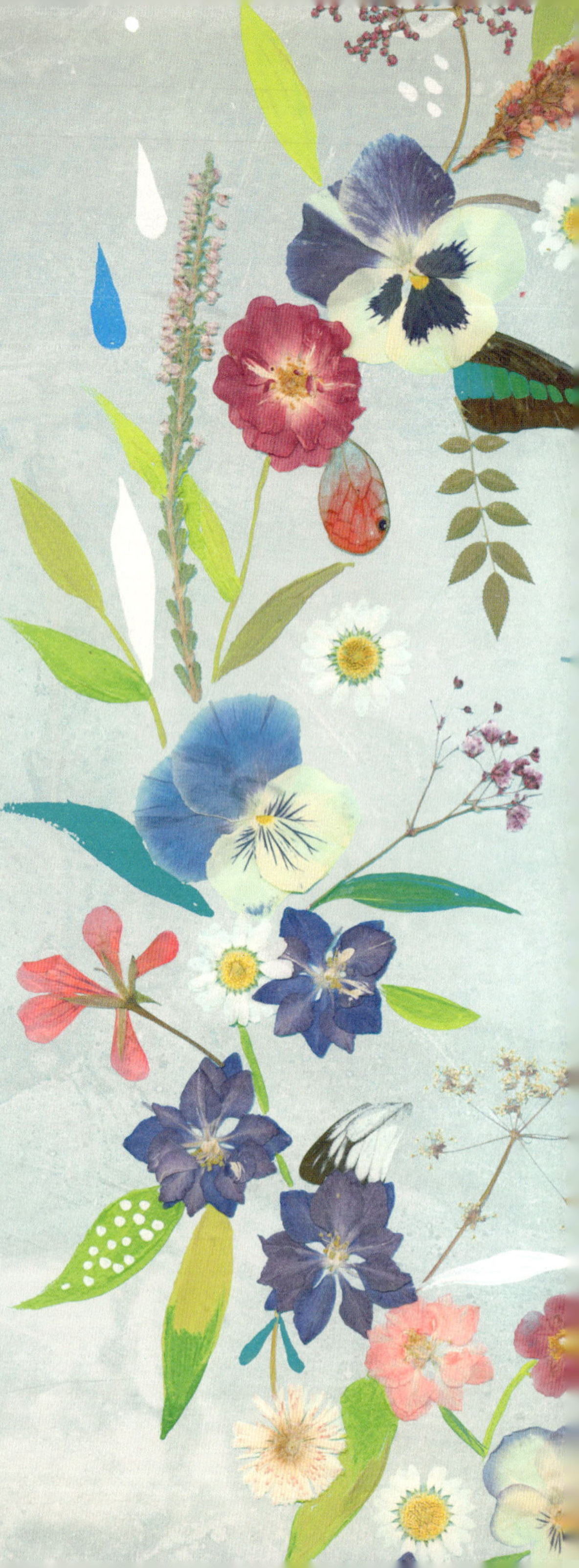

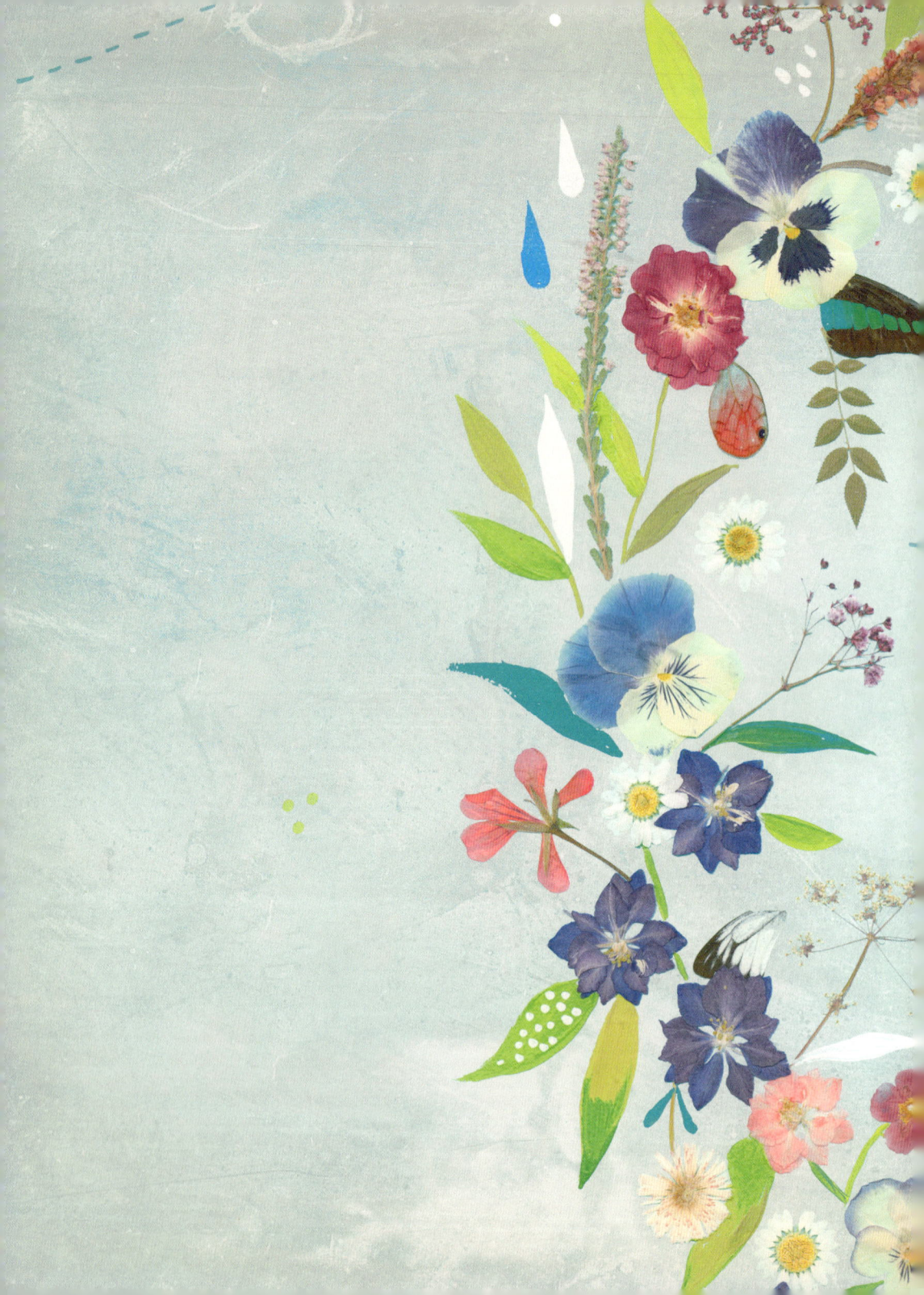

where do you feel most alive?

Pick the first trail through the thick part of the forest, walk until you find a clearing or a meadow. Imagine you've just found your home.

What does it look like?

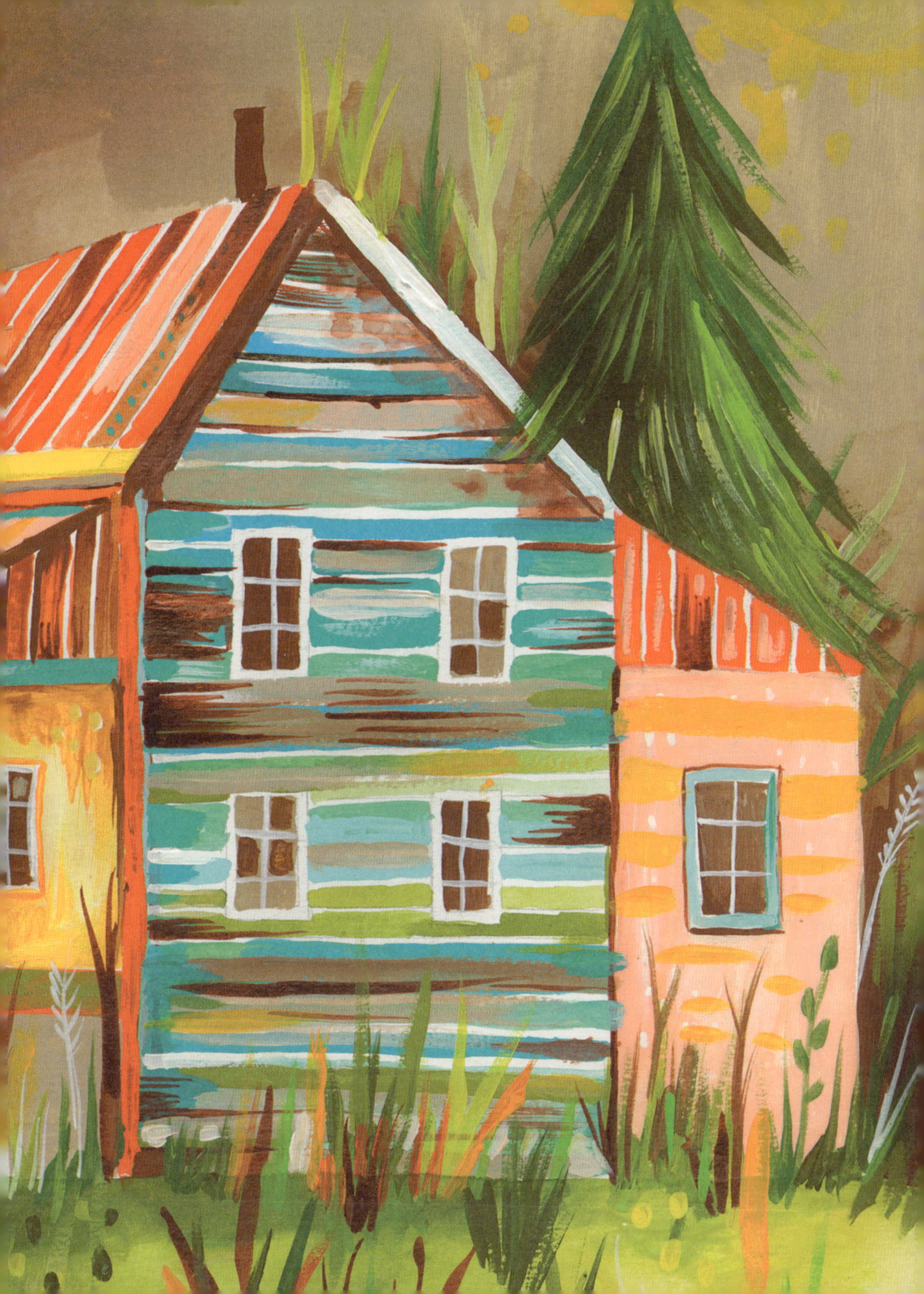

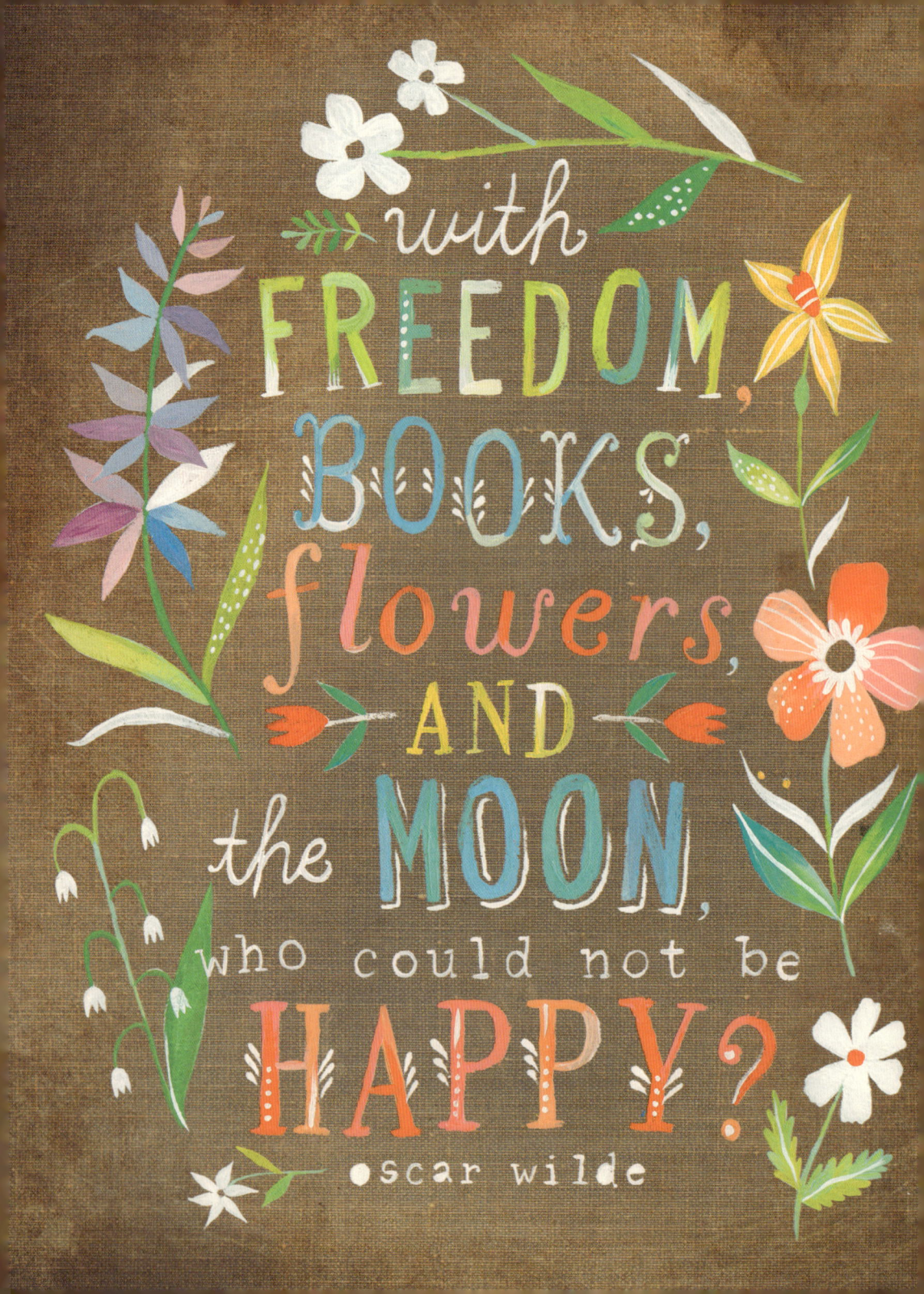

With FREEDOM, BOOKS, flowers, AND the MOON, who could not be HAPPY?

- oscar wilde

With inexpressible delight you wade out into the grassy sun-lake, feeling yourself contained on one of Nature's most sacred chambers, withdrawn from the sterner influences of the mountains, secure from all intrusion, secure from yourself, free in the universal beauty. And notwithstanding the scene is so impressively spiritual, and you seem dissolved in it yet everything about you is beating with warm terrestrial human love, delightfully substantial and familiar. — John Muir —

SKETCH AT AN OUTDOOR CAFÉ WITH A CUP OF CHAMOMILE TEA.

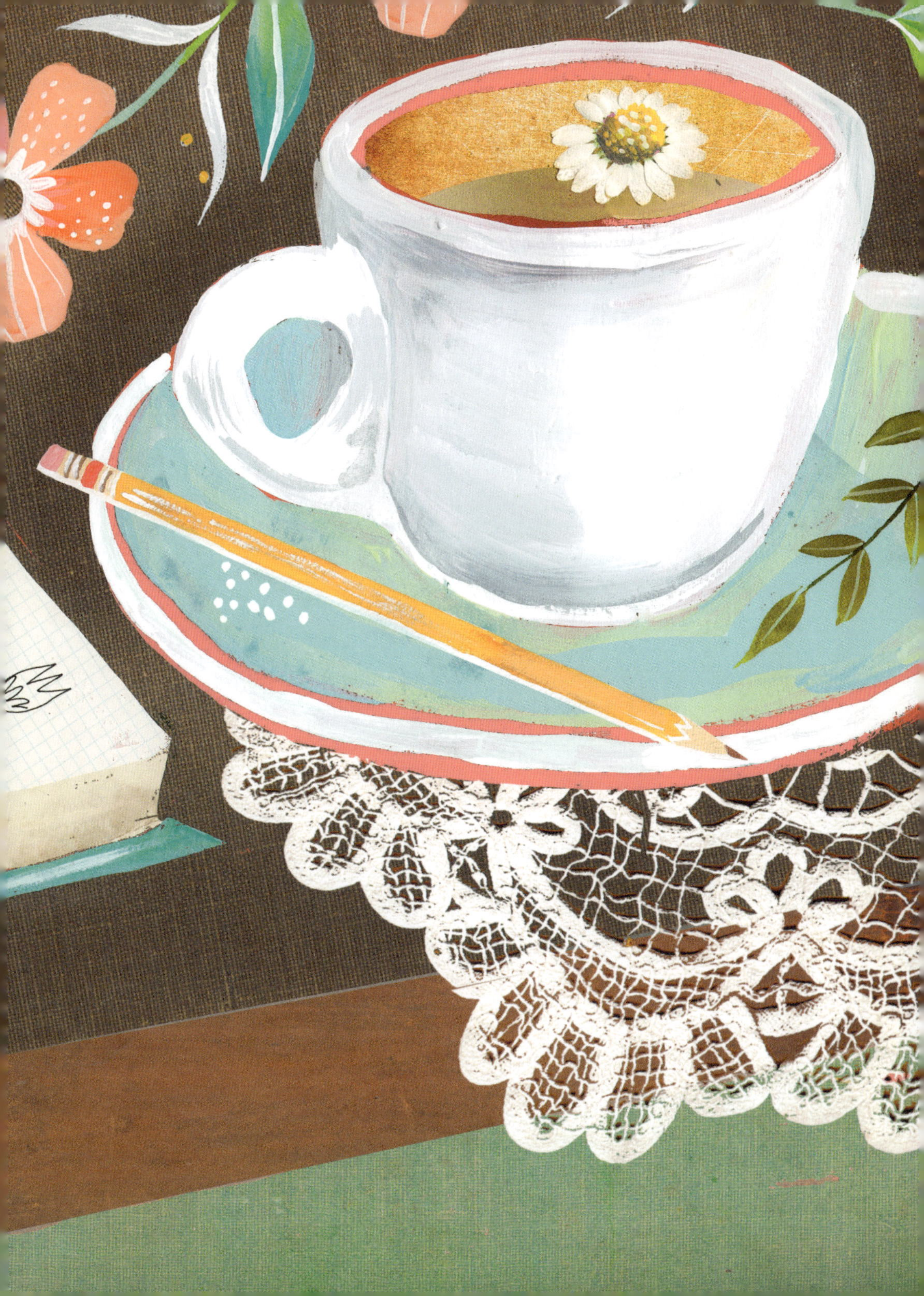

Describe the most beautiful place you've ever been

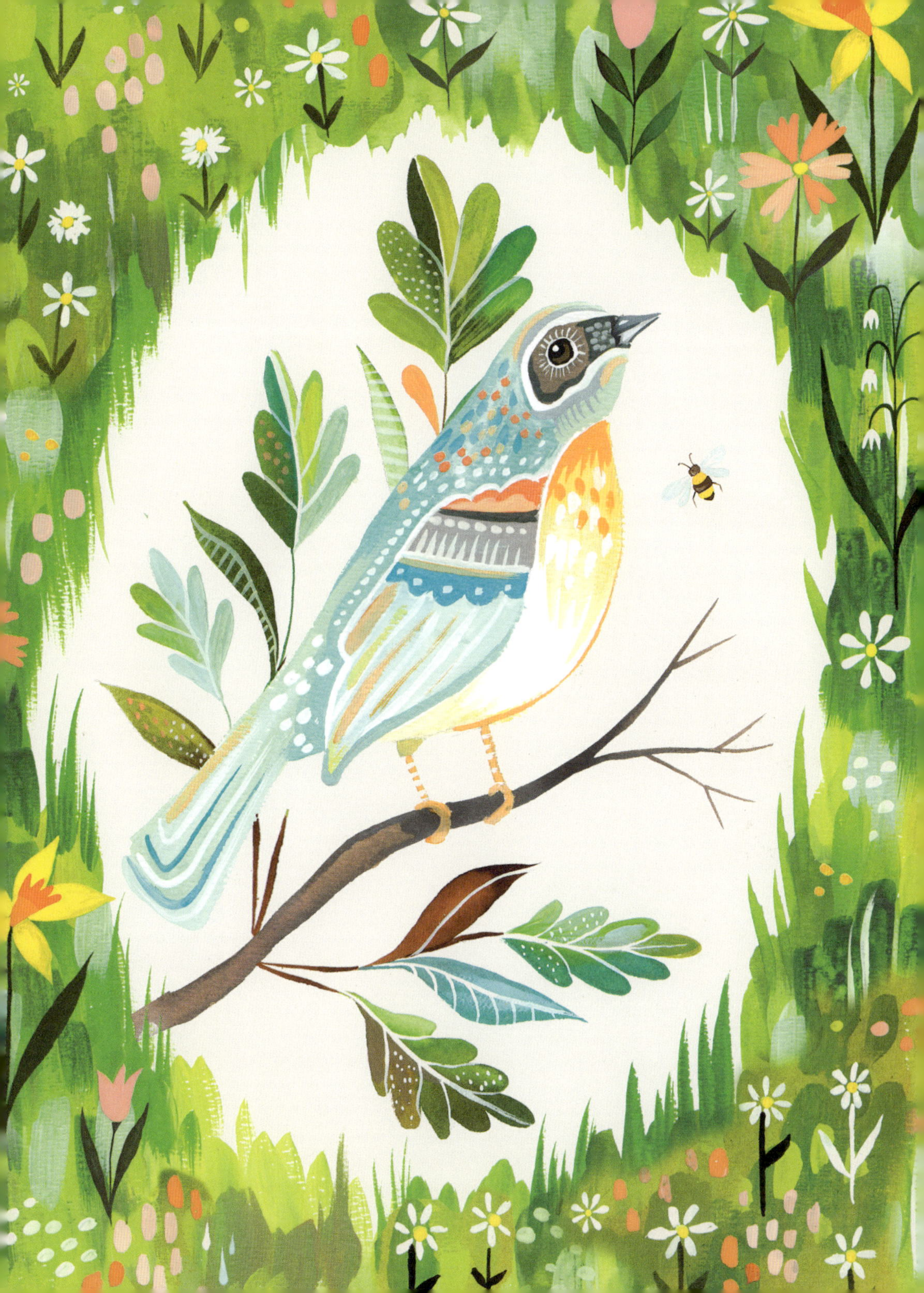

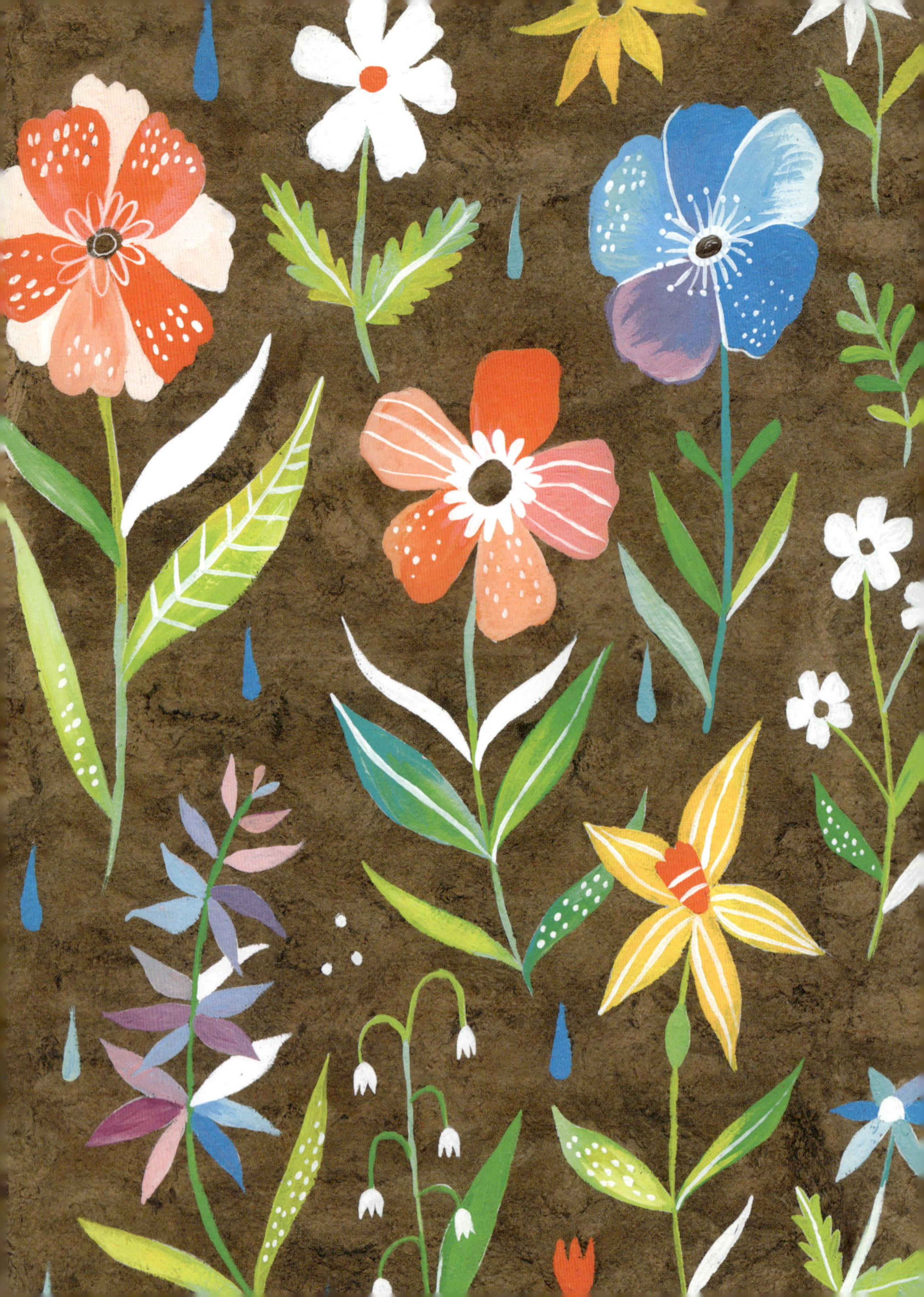

IF YOU'RE
A PAINTER,
TRY USING
WATER FROM
THE SEA
OR RIVER.
IT WILL ADD
A SWIRL OF
MAGIC TO
YOUR ART.

FIND A SUN-WARMED SPOT IN THE WOODS AND DISSOLVE INTO THOREAU'S WALDEN

Sometimes, in a summer morning, having taken my accustomed bath, I sat in my sunny doorway from sunrise till noon, rapt in a revery, amidst the pines and hickories, and sumachs, in undisturbed solitude and stillness, while the birds sing around or flitted noiseless through the house, until by the sun falling in at my west window, or the noise of some traveller's wagon on the distant highway, I was reminded of the lapse of time.

— Henry David Thoreau

GAZE UPON A CLOUD-FILLED SKY. DRAW WHAT YOU SEE.

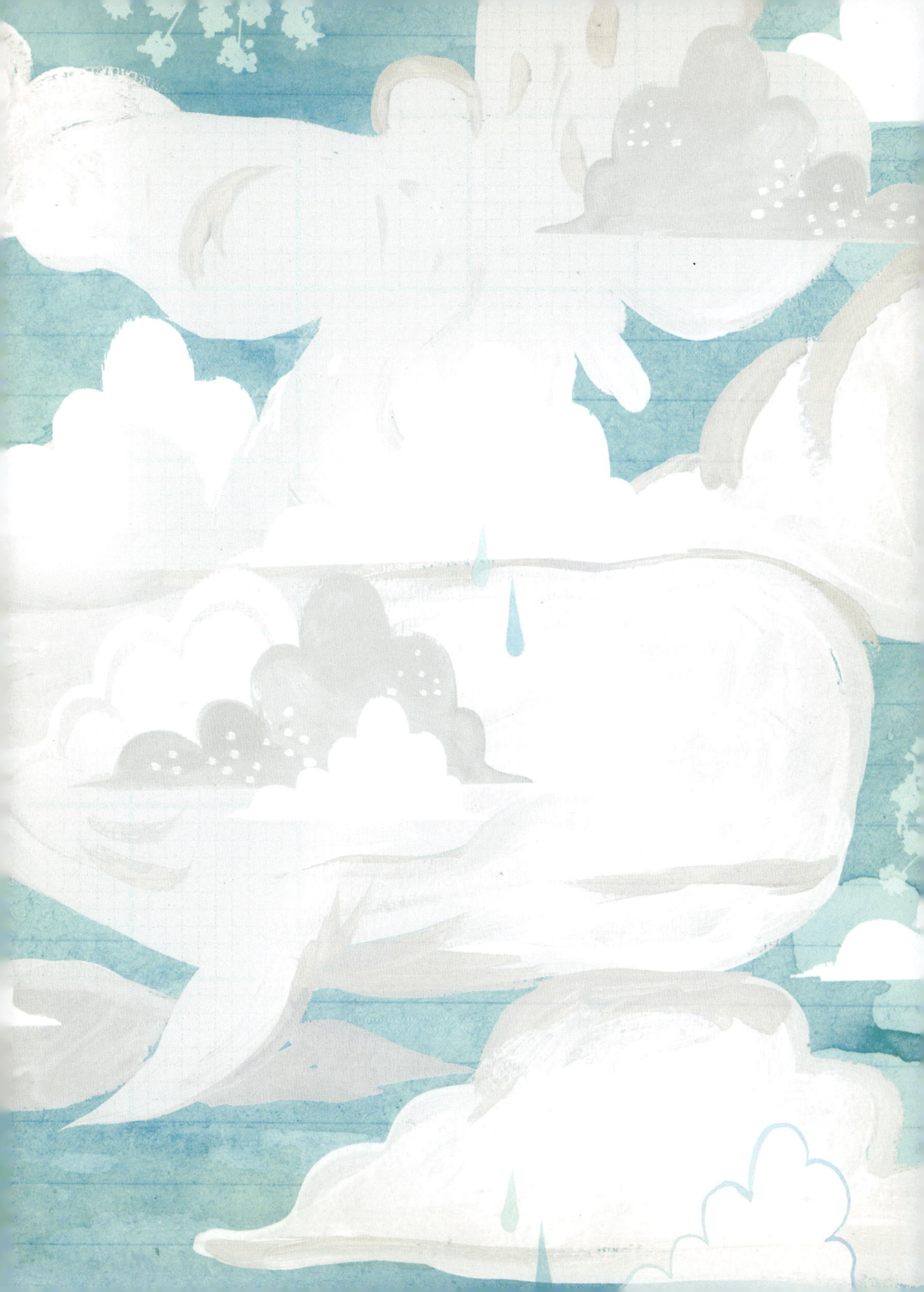

Weather Folklore

The higher the clouds, the better the weather.

Clear moon, frost soon.

Rainbow at noon, more rain soon.

Cold is the night when the stars shine bright.

Trout jump high when a rain is nigh.

A sunshiny shower won't last an hour.

The daisy shuts its eye before rain.

If you see toadstools in the morning, expect rain by evening.

Birds flying low, expect rain and a blow.

A single magpie in spring, foul weather will bring.

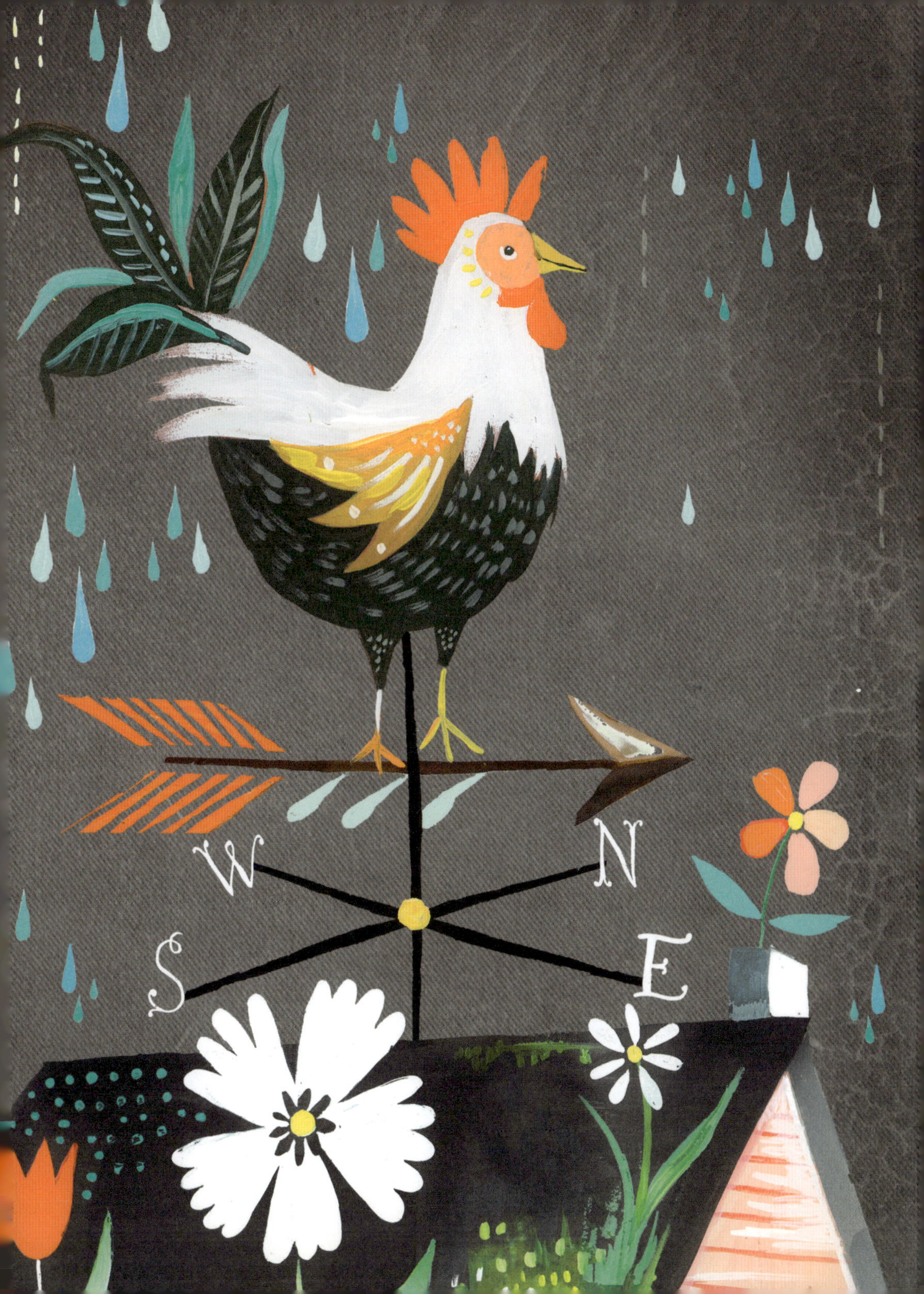
W
N
S
E

Always maintain a kind of Summer even in the middle of Winter

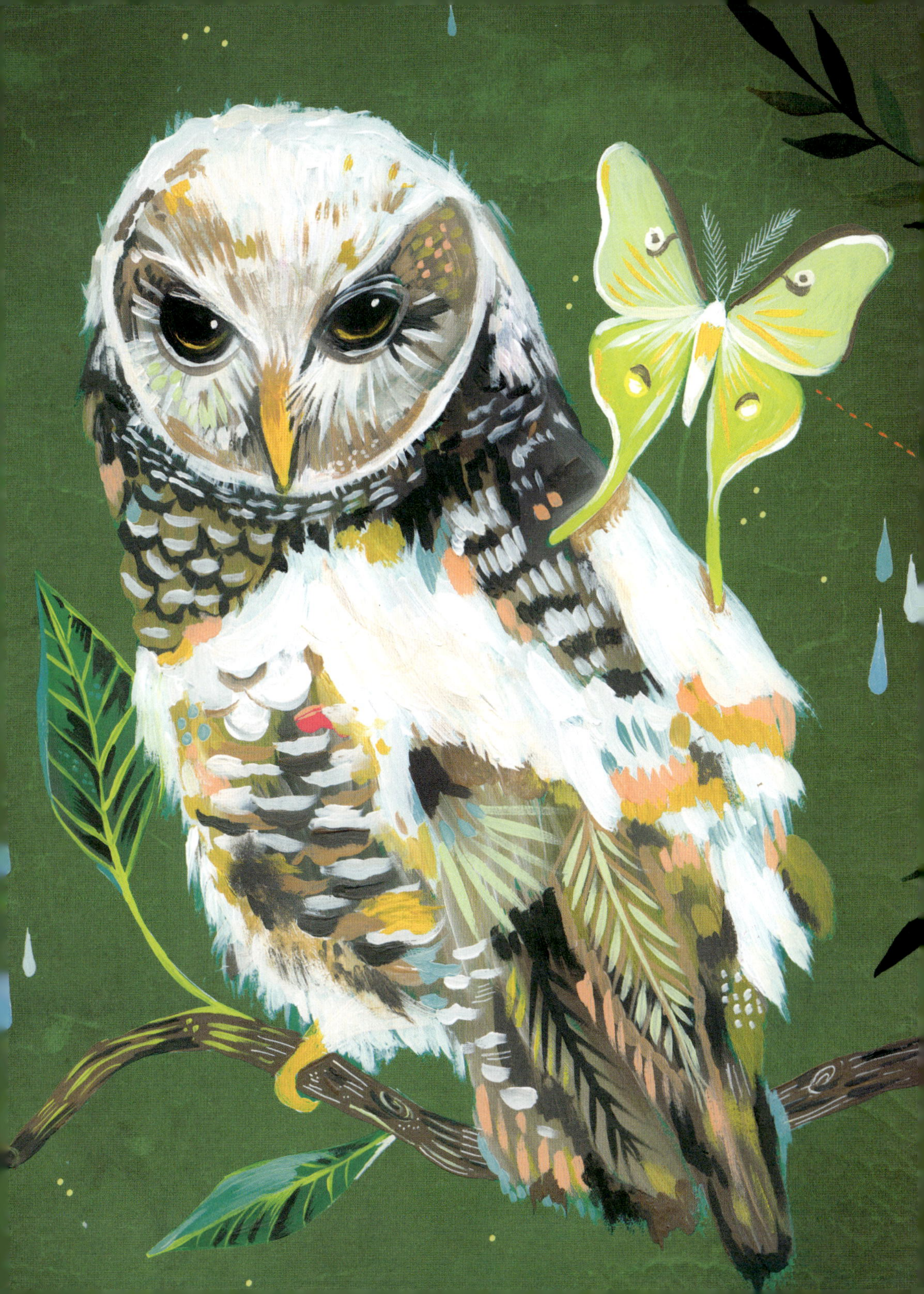

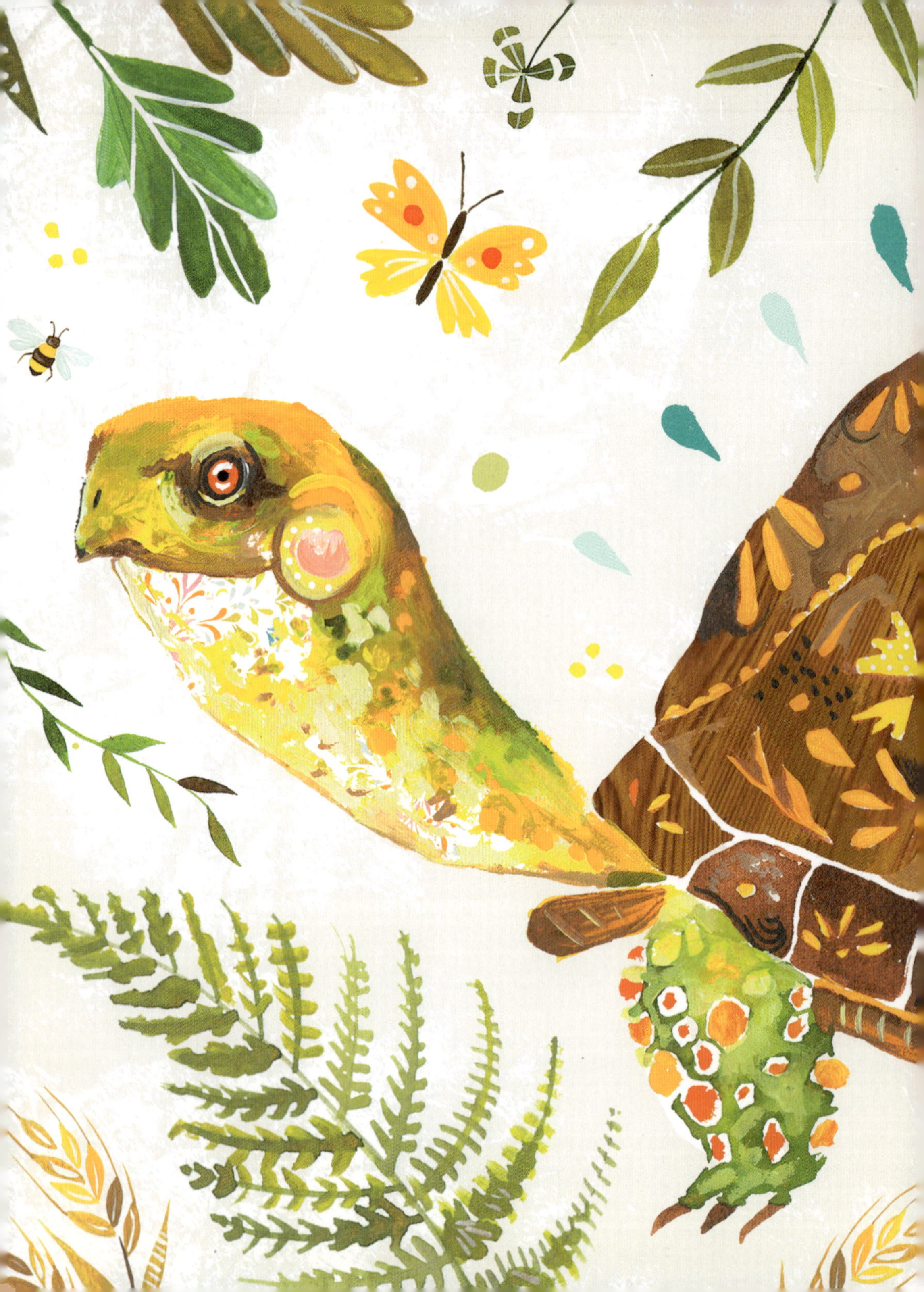

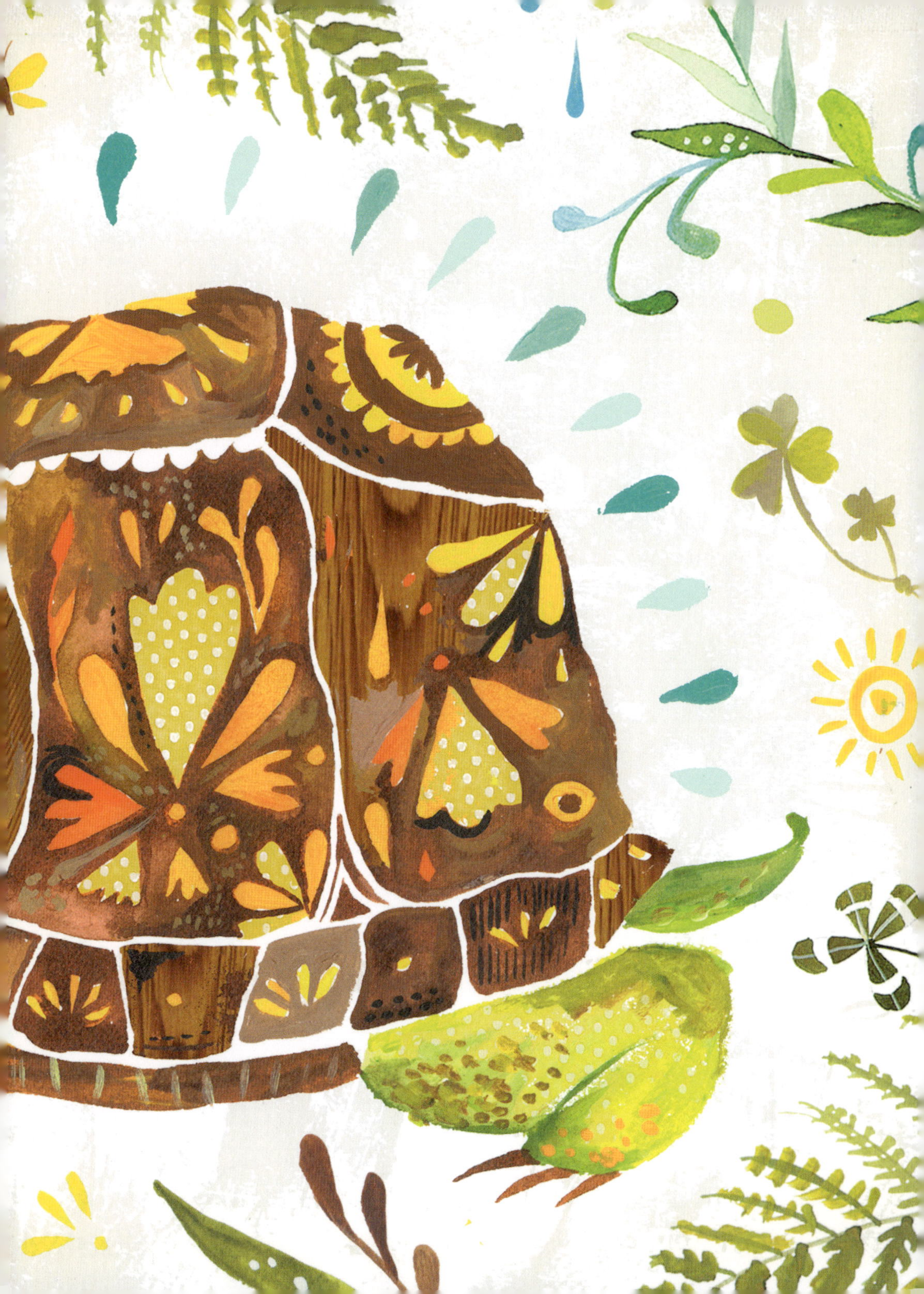

It is the sweet, simple things of life which are the real ones after all.

—Laura Ingalls Wilder

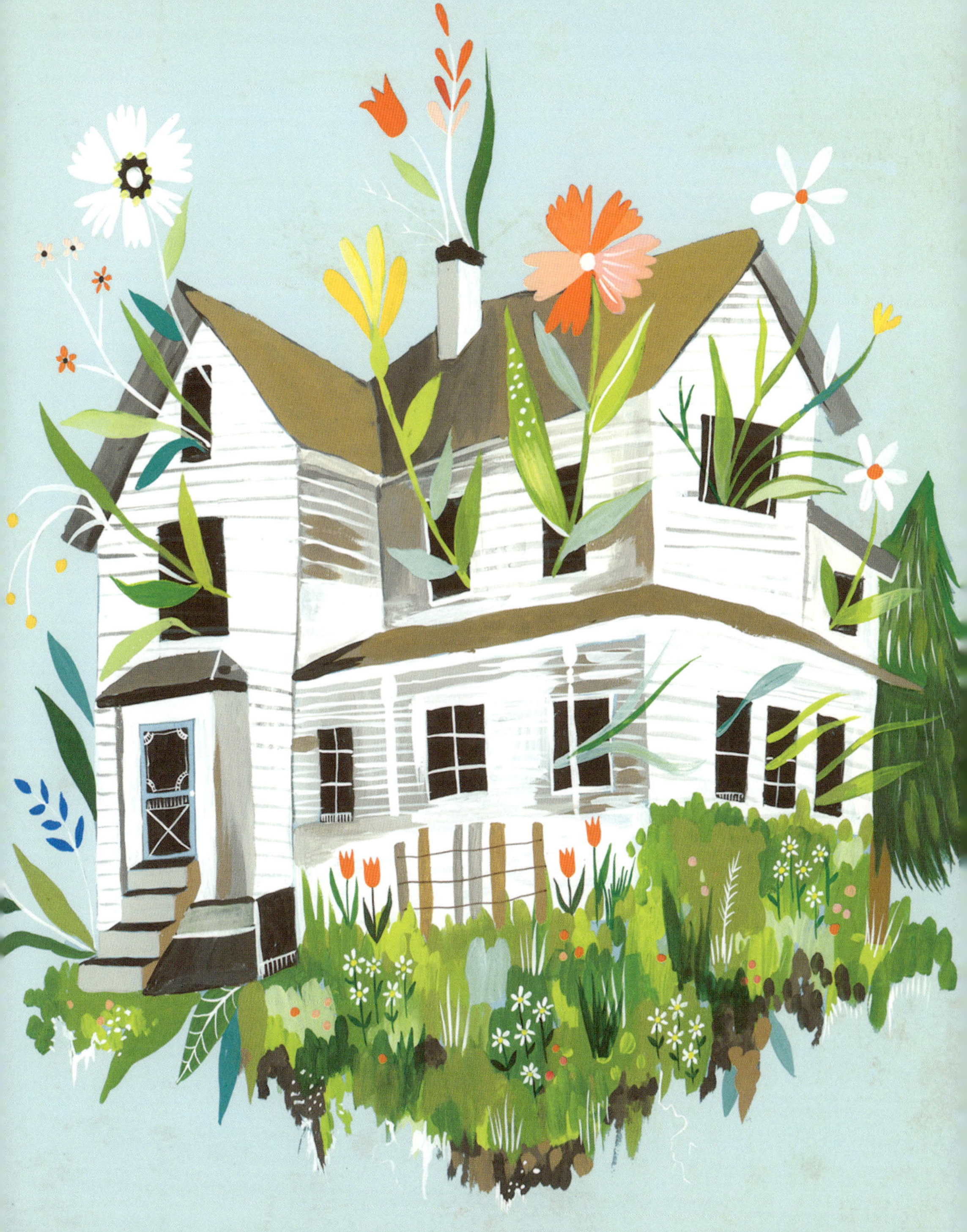

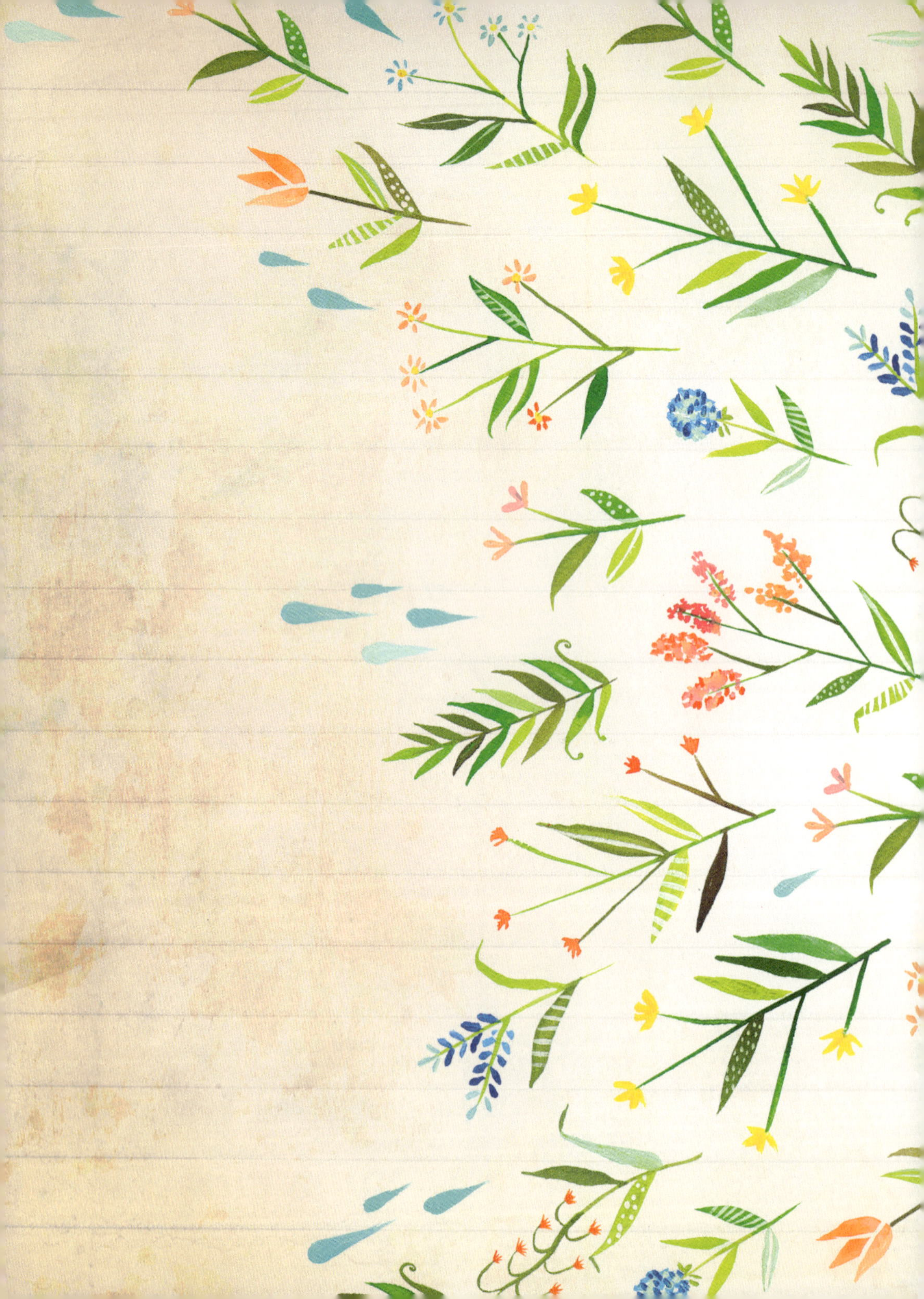

The trees began to whisper and the wind began to roll and in the wild March morning I heard them call my soul

—Alfred Lord Tennyson

wonder of it

e DER all

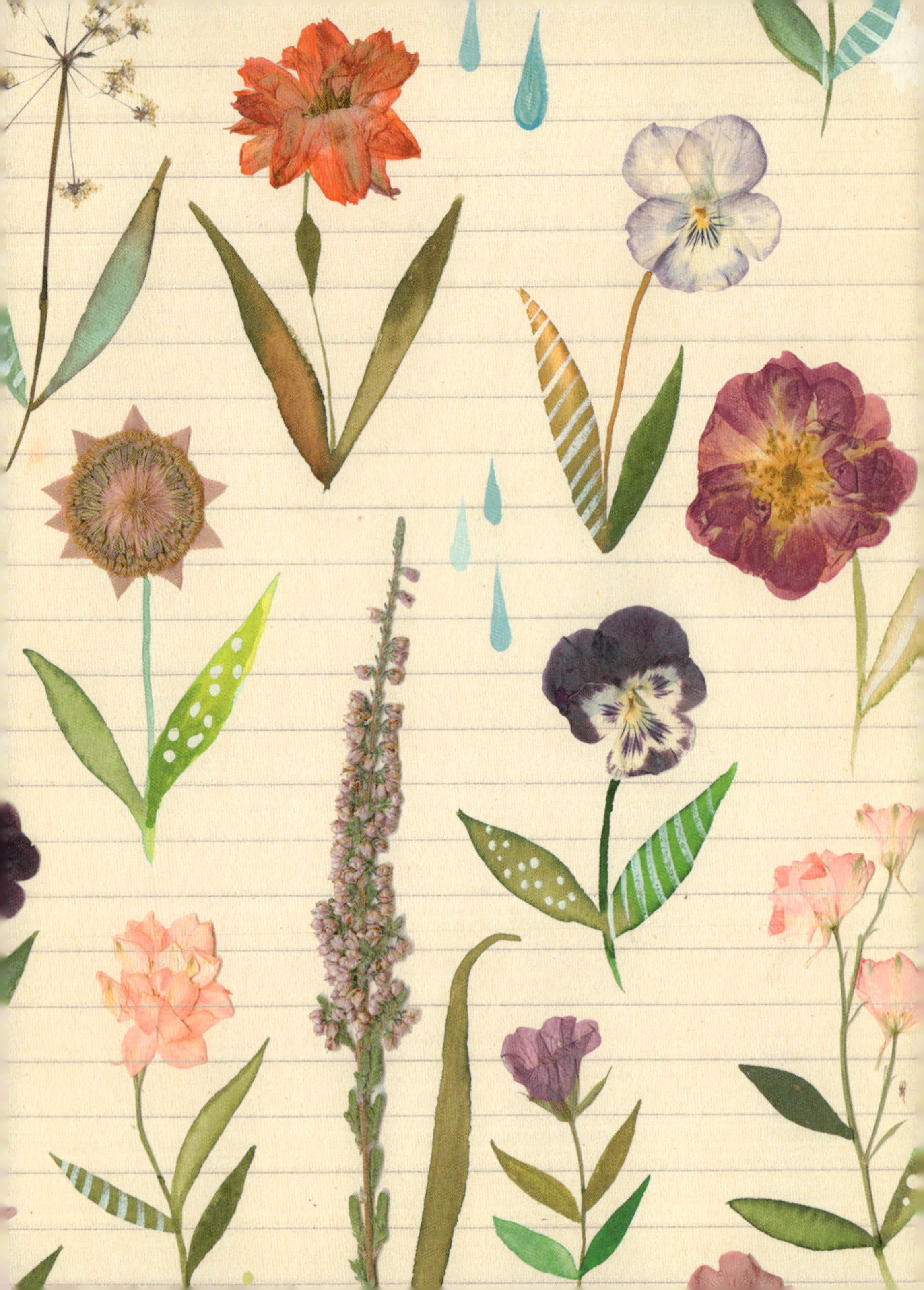

acknowledgments

To my love Elijah, for his support, affection, and delicious cooking. To my sweet baby Finn Orion, born in the middle of this project, who inspires me to look at the world with eyes of wonder. To my mom, Laurie, and my dad, Sam, for raising me with the utmost care & love in the fields, encouraging me to follow my heart and teaching me how important nature is for the soul. To my brother, Robby, an enormous inspiration who I will always see as an explorer, seeking to ever-fully understand the secrets of the universe. To Brian, for encouraging me with his work ethic, love for the land, and dedication to our family.

To my business mentor and dear friend, Betsy Cordes, for keeping me on track, and offering a never-ending flow of motivation, encouragement, and inspiration. Special thanks to Chuck Cordes for his work gathering permissions for the many quotations that appear in this book. Thank you to my dear friend Gabriel Edwards for helping me form ideas, edit, and stitch together my ramblings. To Alia, for her wisdom and knowledge surrounding self-care, to the Irwin family for their support and love. A very special thanks to Melanie for keeping my print shop afloat so I have time and freedom to paint.

I have so much gratitude for everyone who has contributed to my undying wanderlust and many adventures. You know who you are. Without you this book would not be possible.

Katie Daisy, a self-proclaimed wildflower, is an artist whose paintings capture the essence of living in harmony with nature. Katie lives and works in a quiet cabin in Bend, Oregon, with her husband and son.

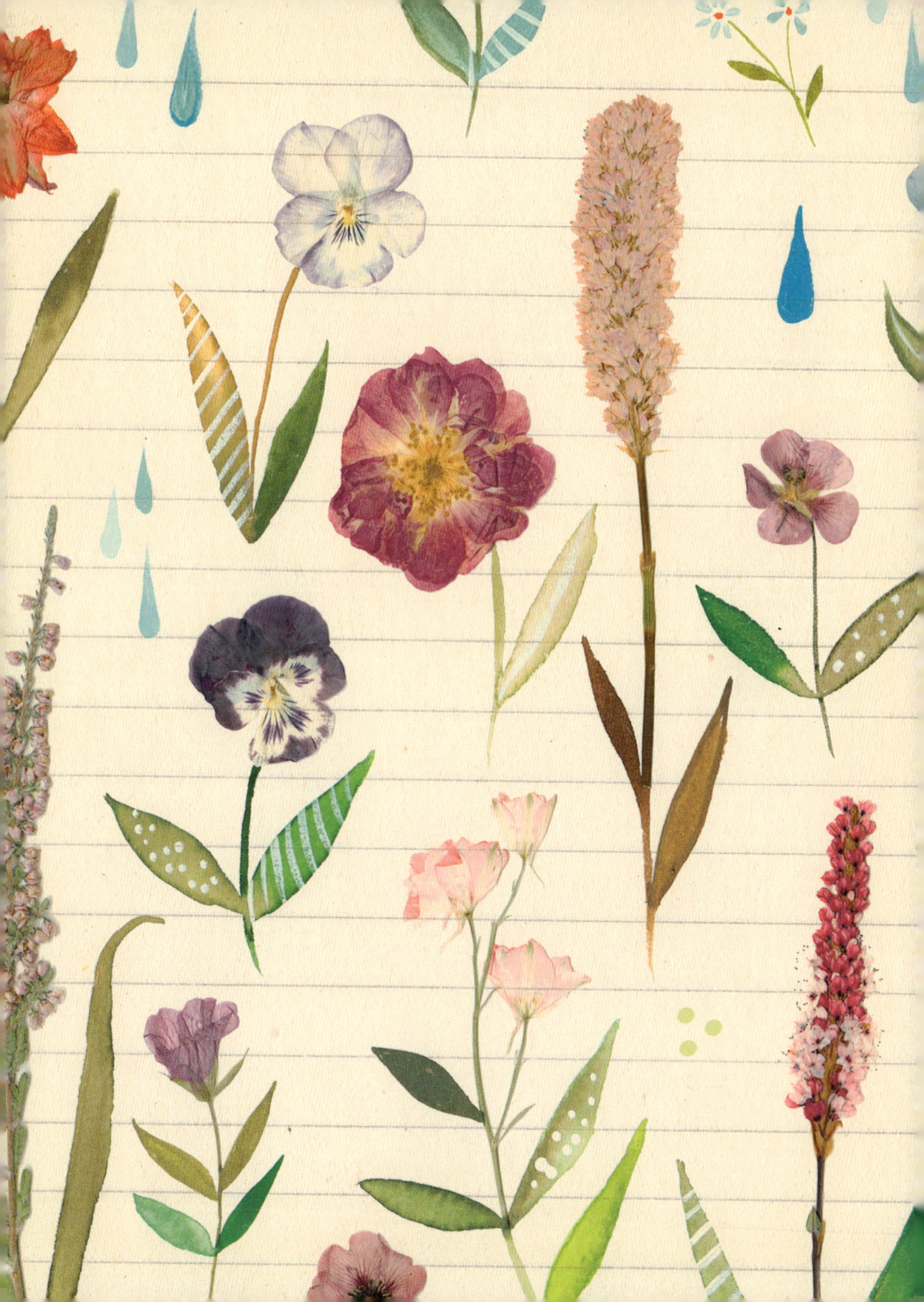

If you have enjoyed this book
or it has touched your life in some way,
we would love to hear from you.

Please send your comments to:
Hallmark Book Feedback
P.O. Box 419034
Mail Drop 100
Kansas City, MO 64141

Or e-mail us at:
booknotes@hallmark.com

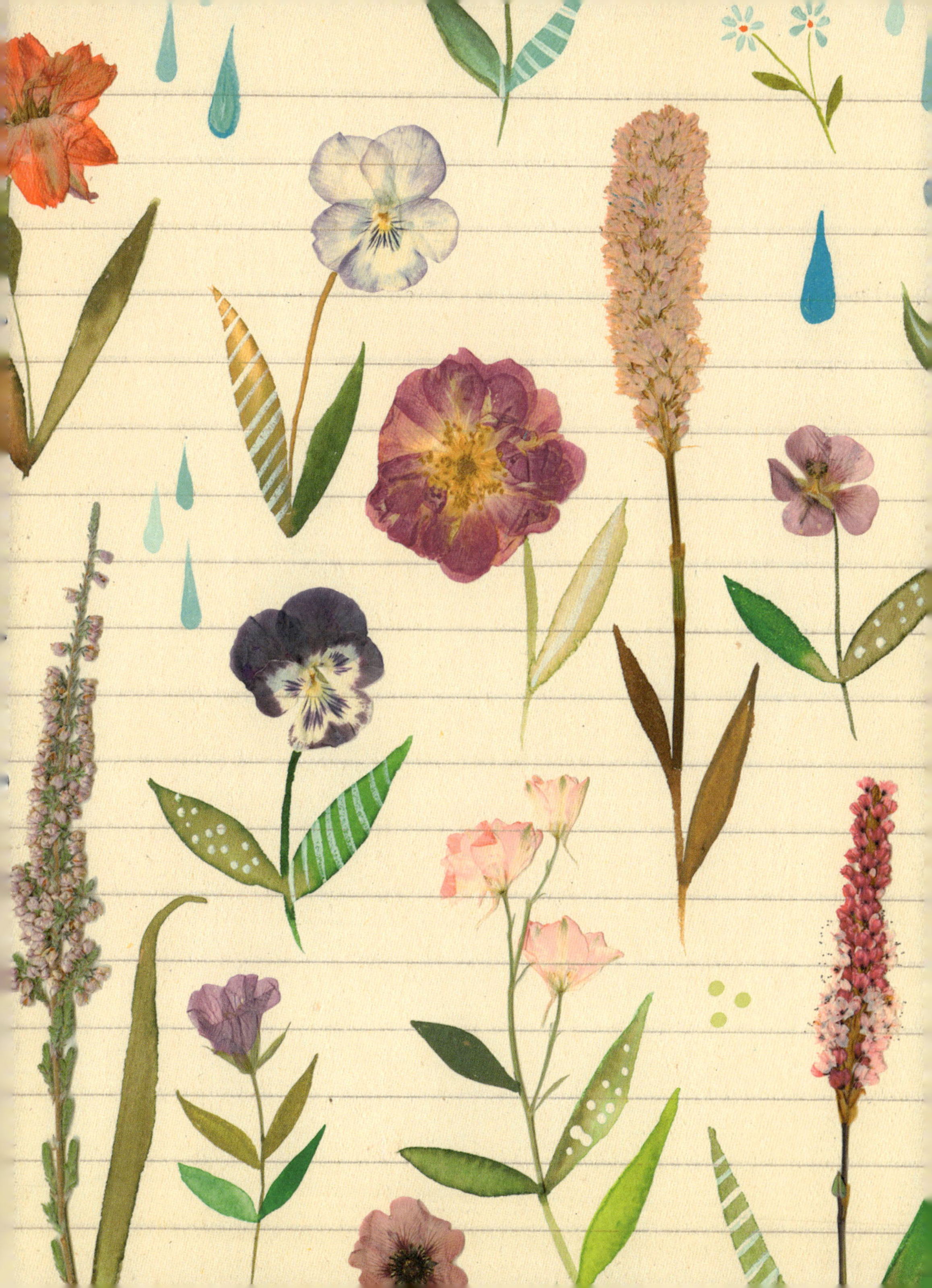

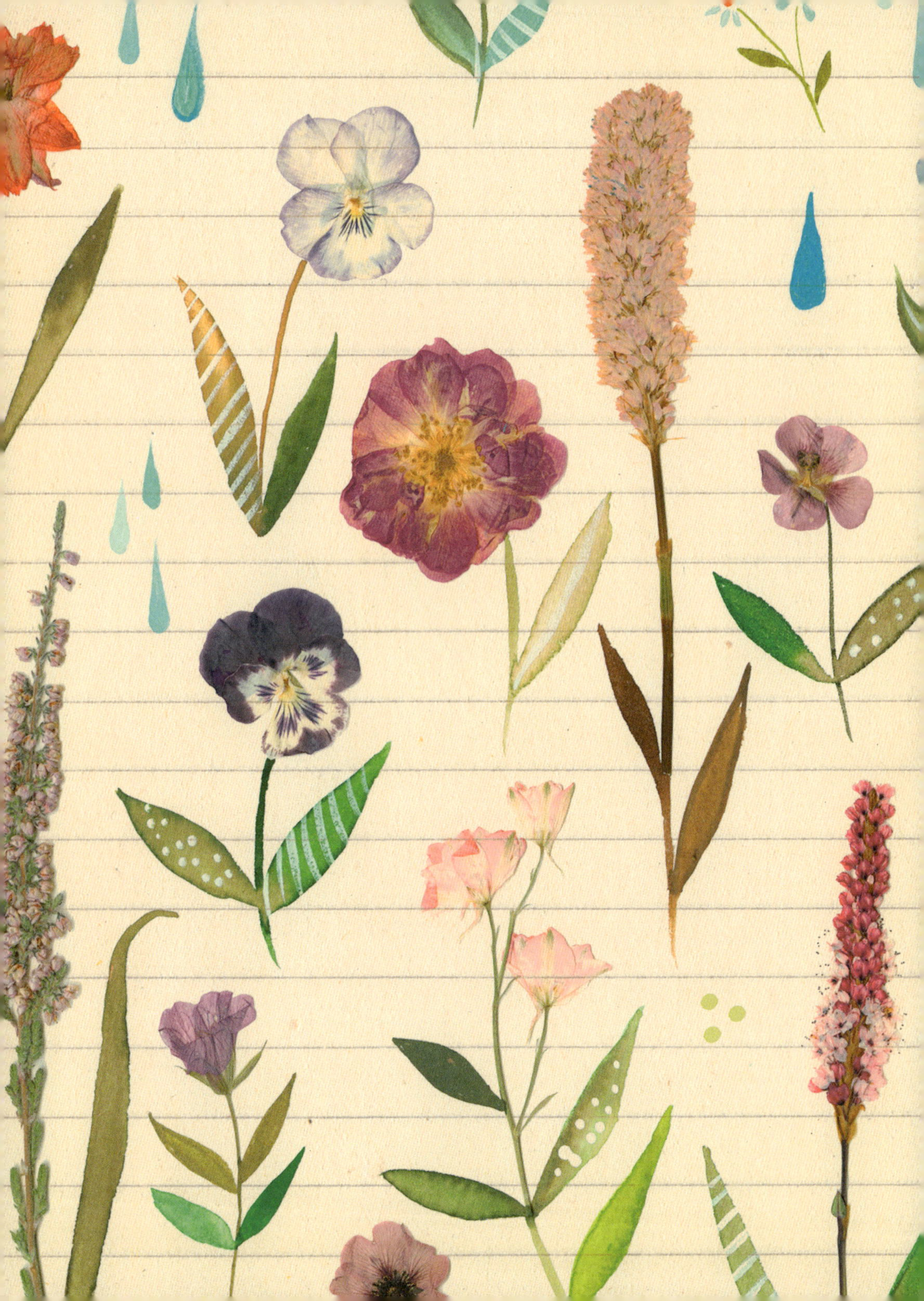

a Gift For:

From:

To Heather Bee,
the most wild of all flowers.

Copyright © 2016 by Katie Daisy.

This edition published in 2016 by Hallmark Gift Books, a division of Hallmark Cards, Inc., Kansas City, MO 64141 under license from Chronicle Books.

Visit us on the Web at Hallmark.com.

All rights reserved. No part of this book may be reproduced in any form without written permission from the publisher.

ISBN: 978-1-63059-868-6
BOK1314

Made in China
0117